Glyn Marston is a man who took on the most gruelling challenges on foot to become a huge name in the world of ultra-distance running. Despite being on medication for life to control epilepsy, he went on to conquer challenges such as running 150 miles nonstop and across the Grand Canyon.

It was no surprise that he would raise thousands of pounds for charities from his gruelling endeavours.

Glyn Marston

THE RISE AND FALL OF AN ULTRA-DISTANCE RUNNER

AUSTIN MACAULEY PUBLISHERS™

LONDON • CAMBRIDGE • NEW YORK • SHARJAH

A CIP catalogue record for this title is available from the British Library.

ISBN 9781398404175 (Paperback)
ISBN 9781398404182 (ePub e-book)

www.austinmacauley.com

First Published (2021)
Austin Macauley Publishers Ltd
25 Canada Square
Canary Wharf
London
E14 5LQ

Sneyd Striders running club with a special thanks to:

Nigel Churchill, Steve Hill, Jill Hill, Dick Johnson, Simon Kimberley, Trevor Simms, Stan Harrison, Sean Haydon, Colin Highfield, Ken Highfield, Geoff Farnell, Ian Hill.

Vicki Michelle of BBC TV's *'Allo 'Allo!* for her words of encouragement and continued support.

Asics UK for their sponsorship.

Chris Chittell and Tony Audenshaw of ITV's Emmerdale for their encouragement and for sharing a few marathon moments together.

Lilywhites in Picadilly for supporting the world treadmill record attempts.

ITV News Central, BBC's *Midlands Today* (Nick Owen in particular) and local newspaper *Express and Star* for getting the stories out there and helping to boost the fundraising.

Louise and Liam Marston, who never complained when their father was away on running challenges.

Ann Marston (ex-wife), who became a widow to running and, despite differences in their marriage, became totally supportive throughout.

Table of Contents

Introduction

I suppose there comes a point in everyone's life when you look back at your past and think, *Did I really do that?* And I guess that everyone has a story to tell but my story shouldn't have really happened, I guess.

As a man who is on medication to control childhood epilepsy, my life should be one of trying to lead an ordinary life, but for me, my life was to be extraordinary and I would find myself taking on some of the most gruelling challenges that a man could face on foot.

After being diagnosed with epilepsy in 1977, my life was never to be the same again, there was the pain, the heartache and the stress of having an illness I didn't quite understand – and why me? However, I lived through it and eventually (after quitting smoking) became a long-distance runner and ran across the Grand Canyon, and ran in races of 150 miles, but more importantly raised thousands of pounds for charity.

My life as a well-known, ultra-distance runner was to show me as a fit person and does not reflect my health as a teenager and my story from being a teenager with epilepsy, right through to becoming a local hero, fundraising champion and a prolific name in the world of ultra-distance running is a testament to my strength of mind as well as my stamina.

This is my story of taking on challenges in life as well as in sport, going beyond all expectations and running in marathons and beyond.

Chapter One
As It Began

I find myself lying on a hospital bed, recovering from an operation to completely replace my damaged right knee, lying in a hospital ward and having time to contemplate on my life as one of Britain's most prolific runners in the ultra-distance running scene at that time (that particular time, ultra-distance running had fewer participants than now).

I had broken many world records for running on a treadmill, had my name mentioned in many sports magazines, been featured on television quite a few times and was featured on a BBC documentary.

As I lay on my bed, I stared at the heavily bandaged knee, there were traces of blood that had seeped through the dressing that dominated my (now) titanium right knee, but I could feel no pain at all (this was due to the fact my right leg had been injected with a nerve block that had been given to me to numb the pain that would be too excruciating to bear following an operation to completely replace my knee).

As I lay there feeling groggy from the operation, a nurse walked up to my bed, "Hello Glyn, how are you feeling after your operation?" I greeted the nurse as she sat next to my bed, "You are so young to have had this kind of operation, what have you been doing to yourself young man?" she asked.

"Well," I replied, "if you have got the time to listen, I have got the time to tell you," I continued.

My story should begin back in 1993 when I quit smoking but I guess I should go back a little further than that…

I met Ann at work, she was my supervisor at the time and being five years older than me, it was amazing that I had 'pulled' a woman at the age of seventeen years. At the age of nineteen, I asked Ann if we could live together. I was in an overcrowded house with five sisters, which meant a long queue each morning for the bathroom (and one sister in particular would deliberately take her time to hold the rest of us up). Ann was not getting on too well with her mother and so we decided to rent a flat together.

After a few years of living together, we decided to get married, the date was to be December the tenth, 1983, just two days after my twenty first birthday – well, it was supposed to be my birthday party but somehow it got turned into a wedding reception.

It was a cold day and everyone turned up at Walsall registry office chilled to the bone, it was like a production line with one couple being married and us waiting to be married and another couple waiting in the same waiting room to be wed after us.

After a few years, we decided to try for a baby and Ann was pleased to announce her pregnancy, but the joys of becoming parents didn't last too long when Ann called me at work from the anti-natal clinic in floods of tears.

I was still working at the same warehouse which was only down the road from the clinic, and on arrival I was told that they thought the baby that Ann had been carrying for almost six months may have died.

The days that followed saw us going to hospital for Ann to have another scan and it was confirmed that our baby was dead and Ann would have to deliver it herself.

We were in turmoil, devastated, as it appeared our whole world had come to an end – the one thing we had hoped for had been taken from us and the feeling of emptiness would never be filled. After carrying a baby for almost six months, the hope of parenthood was almost certain until the moment that Ann was having a scan and the nurse confirmed that the baby Ann was carrying was dead, Ann was to stay in hospital until she had delivered our deceased baby.

I couldn't eat and I definitely couldn't sleep so I lay on the settee with my head phones on listening to Queen (as I always did in times of stress). I recently bought a new album by Queen which was titled 'The works' and featured the chart topping 'Radio Ga-Ga', but again a track sprang into my mind that was so poignant to the current situation and that track was 'Is this the world we created' which had lyrics such as "… You know that everyday a helpless child is born, who needs some loving care inside a happy home…", so apt at that time I can tell you – I would eventually fall asleep on the settee and wake up just in time to get dressed for work and calling the hospital to check on my wife. It was Ann's decision that I carried on going to work, as sitting at her bedside waiting for the end of this terrible chapter to end would only add to the melancholy.

The week was spent with me going to work then rushing off to the hospital in a taxi to visit Ann, for I hadn't taken my driving test and I had sold my motorbike.

On a Friday evening, I went to visit Ann and she told me that she had given 'birth' to a girl and that our ordeal was now over, we just fell into each other's arms as the tears just flowed as Ann was glad that the nightmare for her was over but obviously sad that our chance of being parents had now gone.

Saturday morning, I woke up only when I fell out of bed and was flat out on the bedroom floor, it was 11 am and I had over slept.

I had missed several phone calls and numerous knocks on the door as I had slept like a rock, I had no time to lose as I had to collect Ann from the hospital in a taxi.

It was good to have Ann back home but it was like treading on eggshells as I tried to protect Ann from anything that was 'baby' related, and isn't it funny that almost every television programme had a baby theme in it, eventually the hurt got less and less over time.

After a year had gone by, we decided to try again and Ann was extra careful throughout her pregnancy; we even quit smoking together to ensure we had a healthy baby.

We could not agree on a boy's name as Ann wanted 'Matthew' and I wanted 'Aaron' or 'Audie' after my brother. Ann was adamant that the name Audie was out of the question as one Audie Marston in the world was enough, however we did agree on 'Louise' for a girl.

Ann was overdue and was taken to hospital to be induced into labour, and on the morning of Monday the 13th of October, I arrived at the hospital as I wanted to be present for the birth of my child.

However, Ann could not be induced into labour so we had to wait for her to go into labour by herself. I spent almost three days at the hospital as I didn't want to miss the birth of my baby, Ann went into labour and she was put into a side room with her contractions being monitored. Ann was eventually taken into the delivery room as her contractions became more frequent, and the start of parenthood was almost here.

But Ann's contractions started to get slower and the baby was showing signs of being distressed, so the decision was made to give Ann an emergency caesarean.

At 3:10 pm on Wednesday, the 15th of October 1986, my daughter 'Louise' was born and as Ann was still in theatre, I was holding my baby girl in my arms, with tears in my eyes. I couldn't believe what we had created – a beautiful little girl.

Fatherhood suited me well for I had finally grown into a responsible and caring man, and each Sunday morning I would walk the two miles to my parents' house pushing Louise in her pram to show off my beautiful little girl, however, myself and Ann had starting smoking again but we didn't smoke near Louise.

Louise grew up to be a proper 'daddy's girl', she liked everything that her daddy liked, programmes such as 'Only fools and horses', 'men behaving badly', and 'Red Dwarf'. She even listened to my music with me and became a huge fan of Freddie Mercury and Queen.

By now I was taking driving lessons and put in for my driving test quite quicker than expected, and on the 2nd of

January 1990 (the first working day of the new year) I passed my driving test to the delight of my family.

It was when Louise was four and a half years old that Liam was born, again myself and Ann could not agree on a boy's name – I wanted Liam for a boy and Terri for a girl, but Ann was in total disagreement to my choices.

As before, we quit smoking when we knew of Ann's pregnancy and this time we would quit for good (hopefully)!

By now I had left my warehouse job and was working for 'Gateway' which was later to be called 'Somerfield', and Ann got herself a part time job there too, working three evenings a week (four hours each evening).

Ann was given a job working on the checkouts for most of her pregnancy (on my request), then she resumed her usual job on return to work after giving birth.

So near the end of the pregnancy when it was confirmed that Ann would be booked into hospital for another caesarean, we agreed that I would choose the name for a girl and she would choose the name for a boy and that there would be no attempt to try to change each other's minds.

However, on the morning of April the 19th 1991, and a few hours before Ann was due into theatre for the caesarean, another patient gave birth to a baby girl and decided on the name of Stephanie – and Ann fell in love with the name too.

So as Ann was being wheeled out of the ward and up to the theatre, she decided that she will choose the name if we have a girl and I would choose the name if we had a boy and later that same day Liam was born.

As a nurse handed my son to me, I just got so emotional as I held him gently in my arms. "Hey, they hurt your arms when they're young and your heart when the grow up," stated the nurse, what she meant by this was beyond me, perhaps she was trying to tell me that parenthood would have its downs as well as its ups?

November 1991 was a month I would not forget, for my idol and hero 'Freddie Mercury' had died, after months of speculation and 'Tabloid Stories' the obvious had happened – FREDDIE MERCURY WAS DEAD!!

Freddie (so it was rumoured in the national newspapers) had contracted 'HIV', and the rumours were confirmed when Freddie died of an illness bought on by 'AIDS'. A statement written by Freddie Mercury before he died was read to reporters by Brian May which confirmed that Freddie's death was brought on by HIV.

So typical of Freddie Mercury to issue a press statement of his death as to stop the nation's press printing speculation and causing any ridicule for his dedicated Fans.

I was devastated as if I had lost a long-time pal, Queen had been a huge part of my life, for I had been to concerts and spent a lot of cash on Queen Material (records and any memorabilia I could get my hands on). Freddie's death had shocked most of the world and I am sure that millions of fans worldwide were in mourning for a real legend – and like me they would be shedding a tear for the loss of a true entertainer.

On news of Freddie's death, I shut myself in my bedroom and listened to my Queen LP's through my head phones, as I endlessly wiped away the tears that were rolling down my face. Ann had told Louise to leave daddy in peace as he was upset and needed to be alone, but Louise was determined to see if her daddy was okay and burst into my bedroom to hug me.

April 1992, I had managed to get tickets for the 'Freddie Mercury Tribute concert' at Wembley stadium, the show had a star-studded line up and I was there right up to the front of the stage with a few mates paying a last tribute to a real rock legend.

The weekend of the concert was a real buzz for myself and my friends, we had no sleep for almost forty-eight hours, so it was obvious that I slept for almost a whole day afterwards.

Back at home the joys of being a dad was really good, and Liam was growing into a good-looking young lad, well everyone would comment about how he was the spitting image of his dad – so yes, he was growing up to be a great looking.

At nine months old, Liam became ill, it wasn't long after he had his MMR jab that he developed 'flu like' symptoms and was so withdrawn.

The doctor prescribed some antibiotics, but they just gave him sickness and diarrhoea, after only a couple of days of being sick we noticed that Liam's 'soft spot' had swollen and his head was like a huge rugby ball – obviously we rushed him to hospital.

The doctor gave Liam every test imaginable including a lumber punch to test for meningitis,

I heard Liam's scream as I stood outside the theatre with Ann, "That's our son," cried Ann as she struggled to control her tears.

"What are they doing to him," I cried as we fell into each other's arms for some comfort from each other.

We were informed that the lumber punch concluded that Liam had not got meningitis, but the hospital was baffled as to what was wrong with Liam, and after almost a fortnight in hospital it was diagnosed that Liam may have had double pneumonia!

I was angry at the paediatrician for how can she say that he 'MAY' have had double pneumonia – she either knew what illness he had or she hadn't got a clue, but she wouldn't admit to being baffled to Liam's condition.

Ann had slept at the hospital for the whole duration of Liam's ordeal and so when we got Liam back home, there were a lot of making up to Louise to be done, for Louise had never complained once about her little brother having all the attention and that was typical of Louise; so unlike a normal five-year-old, she was blessed with an adult's attitude to life and became so understanding and caring about the situation.

Liam's behaviour had changed since his stay in hospital and we had wondered if he was trying to come to terms with his ordeal in his own little way, perhaps the thought of staying in a strange ward away from the security of his own home had left him a little emotionally scarred and he needed to be reassured that he was safe at home and no-one would take him away to hospital again.

One day at work, I received a phone from Ann, she was sobbing her heart out so much that I had no choice but to go home to calm her down.

She had taken Liam to the local clinic and they were concerned about Liam's lack of reaction to various tests, this was showing signs that there was cause for concern about his mental health.

We watched Liam at play for the few weeks that followed and we could see that he was a little slow in some things that he should have been doing for his age, but we didn't seem to think that it was a huge problem – though the local health authority disagreed with us.

We were invited to a local clinic and we sat there in a room with other doctors, education officials and social workers – we all watched Liam through a 'secret' window.

The blackboard in the room that Liam was playing in was really a window where children would be observed by medics, this was a terrible experience for us both as all the staff were talking about Liam. "He isn't doing this, he isn't doing that." They were all mumbling to themselves as if we weren't there.

"HANG ABOUT A BIT," I shouted, "That's my kid you're talking about," I said, as I lowered the tone of my voice when I realised that the children being observed could hear my shouts.

But the truth was plain to see, Liam wasn't getting involved with activities and was just sitting in the room watching the other kids at play, and to try to deny that there were any problems with Liam would not have helped him in the long term; so we were forced to face the truth that Liam had problems – but what were causing his problems?

Over the coming months, we were told that Liam was showing signs of autism and we would be facing some tough months ahead as he would be observed closely, and less than a couple of years later Liam would be offered a place in a special needs school if his progress hadn't changed by then, this deeply upset Ann and she started to smoke again.

I resisted the smell of nicotine but the craving for a cigarette was becoming stronger each day, and sitting in the same room as my wife who would be smoking was difficult.

One Saturday evening, I went out for a drink with a few work mates and this particular evening was to be the start of a change of lifestyle for me.

As I stood at the bar of a pub in Wolverhampton, I noticed a medal hanging from a shelf behind the bar, the medal was from the London Marathon which was staged a few weeks earlier.

"Is that a London Marathon medal," I asked the barmaid.

"Yes, it's mine," she replied as she plucked the medal from the shelf and placed it around my neck.

I looked at the inscription on the medal which read '1993 London Marathon'.

"I'm going to have one of these next year," I proudly announced as I turned to my drinking buddies.

They all fell about with laughter, "You run the London Marathon, you can't even run a bath," they all jeered.

It was the joke of the night and I got really angry when they all made fun and it wouldn't stop, however I was adamant that next year I would be running in the London marathon.

The next morning, I woke up early and after getting washed I put on a t-shirt and shorts, as I pottered around the bedroom Ann peered over the covers and asked, "What you're doing getting up this early on a Sunday morning?"

"I going for a run," I replied,

"A WHAT?" she shouted as she sat up in bed,

"A run...erm I told my mates that I will run in next year's London Marathon," I said.

Ann screamed with laughter, "LONDON MARATHON, LONDON MARATHON – WHAT'S BOUGHT THIS ON THEN?"

I explained to Ann that with her smoking around me was making me crave for a cigarette, but if I had something to focus on, I could resist the urge to light up, and if I had to face the challenge of being a father of an autistic son, I want to be fit and ready for that challenge, be a champion for my son.

And I was right, for the thought of running on the roads where I lived made me feel like an athlete, and so my new hobby had begun – RUNNING!

A four-mile run, three times a week had turned into six-mile runs, four times a week – then eventually the miles got longer and longer, until I was good enough to go running with a local running club and taking part in 10K races and the odd ten-mile race, until one day I miscalculated a Sunday morning training run and ran just over eighteen miles!

I went out with a group of runners from Sneyd Striders on Sunday morning with the thought of running thirteen miles but after two hours of running, I asked a fellow runner, "How far are we running today?"

To which the reply was, "Eighteen miles or little more."

"Eighteen miles?" I shouted, "But I only wanted to run twelve or thirteen miles," I explained. It seemed that I had ran with the wrong group of runners and these runners were training for a 26-mile marathon and so it had me thinking that I could run the same event too.

Well, I was on a high with my new achievement of running almost twenty miles in one go, and so as I left the group of runners. I headed home and almost sprinted the last few yards down my road.

I ran into the house and announced to Ann that I had ran eighteen miles on my training run, she could not believe me at first but she was delighted that I was progressing so well in my new sport.

Needless to say, that I was now inspired to run in my very first Marathon – a whole 26.2 miles on the 'Robin Hood marathon' in Nottingham.

Chapter Two
The Starting Line

So as I went into training for my first full marathon, I knew that I had to increase the miles and a twenty-mile training run was to be my goal, at work my colleagues were still making fun of me as I would run for six miles in my dinner break and then run home at the end of the day. I was training hard but managed to balance my training with work and family commitments, and so every Tuesdays and Thursdays I would be training with Sneyd Striders Running club (Sneyd pronounced 'Sneed'), and every Sunday morning I would be up with the lark and out running. About three weeks before the Robin Hood marathon in Nottingham, I completed a twenty-one-mile training run which left me exhausted but delighted, as I knew only too well that I would reach the finish line of my first marathon.

Back at home things were getting a little worse, for despite Liam having his problems, Ann was getting fed up of me going out for training runs and I could be up to two hours in one session. She was annoyed with the fact that I would soon be away in Nottingham for a whole day. Eventually, the marathon was upon me and I drove to Nottingham on my own (Ann wasn't really bothered about waiting around for me to run a whole twenty-six miles and a bit). I arrived at the starting area of the marathon and met up with some of my running club mates, such as Trevor, Dick, Stan, Nigel, Sean and Simon.

They were all running in the half marathon and had grave concerns about my ability to run a full marathon, they advised me to run at a steady pace and aim for a finishing time of 'four and a half hours'.

So as I lined up with thousands of other runners, I was getting so excited that I was to be achieving a huge goal in my life and be on course for my true aim to run in next year's London Marathon.

The starting pistol rang out a huge 'BANG' and we are on our way, but jogging for the first mile until the line of athletes thinned out was unavoidable but after that I was into my own pace and enjoying every mile. I was caught up by Sean who advised me that as he was only running the half marathon. I should be a little more behind him if I am to run the full 26.2 miles of the marathon.

Realising that to start off with a pace that is too fast at the beginning would leave me too fatigued towards the finish, I slowed my pace a little and carried on with a 'just enjoy the event' attitude.

The course of the race was a figure eight, whereas the half marathon runners would cut off to the finish line and the marathon runners would carry on and do another 'loop' before returning to the finish line area. This was a low point of the event as some runners were running to the finish line and I had the whole distance to do again, but I just kept myself focused on the second half of the race. I counted each mile as I passed a mile marker and at twenty-three miles, I began to feel the pain of being a long-distance runner, my calf muscles screamed in agony as my quad muscles began to feel heavy.

I was now dragging my feet on the tarmac paths as I tried to keep a continuous pace toward the finish line, but at the twenty-five-mile marker, I could hear the P.A. system at the finish line and someone announcing each runner's name as they crossed the finish line.

I lifted my head and my spirits and picked up my pace as I realised that the end was near, my pace quickened so much that I sprinted the final 200 yards to the finish line and as I heard my name being called over the P.A. system, tears began to fill my eyes as the emotion of completing my first marathon became too overwhelming.

The guys from Sneyd Striders Running club all waited for me at the finish line, and had informed the organisers that it was my first ever marathon and I had only been running for twelve weeks before then, so I was greeted with a huge ovation when I collected my finishers lace panel – yes, all finishers were presented with a frame lace memento from the event instead of the usual medal which was the same size as an LP cover (twelve inches), and made the event well worth running.

I was treated like a hero when my club mates realised that I had finished in a time of 'three hours and fifty-five minutes' instead of the predicted time of four and a half hours. I was ecstatic and exhausted but full of the joys of the event right until I arrived back home some three hours later,

"Look what I've got," I shouted as I walked into the house.

But as Louise snatched my lace panel from me and rushed into the kitchen to show Ann, all Ann could say was, "Is that all you get for running the marathon, hardly worth the effort, they could have given you a medal!"

I wasn't bothered, for they could have given me a cardboard coin just as long as it showed proof that I had ran in my first marathon.

Only a month after the marathon in Nottingham, I received a letter that confirmed that I had a place in next year's London Marathon. I jumped with joy as I couldn't believe my eyes, for many runners don't get accepted in the London Marathon's lottery system, and unless you are an elite runner there is no guarantee of an entry in the event, but I had my entry confirmed – YES!

The training was tough now as the winter months were upon us and wind, rain and snow would provide added resistance to an already gruelling training schedule.

I had decided to run the 1994, London Marathon for a local charity and so came my first ever newspaper interview, and I never thought that I would ever see myself on a page of any newspaper.

My family were excited as were Ann's family about reading my story in the local paper, all the neighbourhood was stopping Ann in the street and asking, "How on earth could Glyn be fit enough to run in the London Marathon?"

Of course the 'celebrity status' that the story gave me was amazing and was fuelling me to do more running and even more training.

My boss at Somerfield arranged my working hours to accommodate my training for the London Marathon which was a huge help, and in return I gave the store some great publicity.

The charity I was to be running for in the London marathon was 'Rainbow House appeal', which was greatly supported by Sheila Tarbuck (our canteen lady and the most wonderful person that I have ever known), and it was because of my respect for Sheila that I had decided to support her in raising funds for the cause.

It soon became the weekend of the London Marathon and I was booked into a hotel with the rest of the Sneyd Striders running club, as we had to collect our race numbers on the Saturday, it would be pointless to travel all the way home then back to London again on the Sunday for the event, so an overnight stay was inevitable which upset Ann. I asked her to come for a weekend away but she refused to leave the children with babysitters for a whole weekend.

After booking into our hotel and having a 'pre-race' evening meal, I climbed into my bed but couldn't go to sleep due to the excitement that was running around in my head. I was tossing and turning in a bid to find that one comfortable spot in bed that would see me nod off to sleep – but my nerves were getting the better of me.

I can't remember what time I actually got to sleep but I woke up earlier than anticipated (again due to my nerves).

After a small breakfast and a few cups of tea, we were all taken by coach to the start line of the marathon and this is where the nervous anticipation started, and as I walked towards the starting area, the butterflies in my stomach got worse.

After trying to control (without success) the butterflies in my stomach, I made my way to the start line along with thousands of other athletes. As the gun went off to mark the start of the marathon, we all just shuffled along the course until the crowd of runners thinned out a little. Just before the first mile marker, I was able to get into my usual pace and begin to soak up the atmosphere from both runners and spectators, this was great as the cheers was endless as onlookers clapped and cheered as we passed.

It wasn't long before the nervous anticipation had baited and I became more relaxed and was able to enjoy the event, running past the 'Cutty Sark' was so thrilling and the crowd that was gathered there was huge, even more so was the cheer that they all generated, it really lifted my spirits and my pace. I was running up 'Jamaica Road' when I took a right turn and there in front of me was 'Tower Bridge' – what a sight. I started to feel a little choked at this point due to the awesome view and the sight of the crowds that were lined against this part of the route. Why Tower Bridge should be such a prominent sight for me on the marathon I don't know, I just became overwhelmed when I realised that I was running over the landmark.

I eventually reached Birdcage walk and just over a mile to the finish line, feeling a little weary, I managed to maintain my pace as the noise from the cheering crowd grew as loud as ever. The last mile seemed to go on forever as the sight of the finish line took ages to come into view but the atmosphere from the crowd was electric and the louder the cheers got, the faster I seemed to be running.

At last the finish line was in sight and my aching legs were to be pushed even more as I sprinted to the finish line, my lungs were about to burst as. I crossed the finish line in a time of three hours and fifty-four minutes – a minute faster than my Nottingham performance, so not a bad performance on the whole.

I returned home with my London Marathon medal worn proudly around my neck, my family were proud of me too – Louise grabbed my medal and wore it around her neck and Ann was congratulating me for sticking to my task by actually running in the London Marathon as promised.

At work, Sheila had collected all my sponsor money and sent it to the charity and in return I was invited to a presentation at 'The Dorchester Hotel' in London with all the other fundraisers for Rainbow House Appeal.

The presentation was for 'The Children of Europe Awards' and was due to be presented by Princess Diana but due to unforeseen circumstances she was unable to attend, so Princess Michael of Kent did the honours of presenting children with awards for unselfish acts of bravery. I went along with Ann who was looking forward to experiencing the high life as we were informed that celebrities will be present at the function, on arrival we couldn't believe our eyes as television celebrities were waiting at the reception area to welcome all guests of the presentation.

I was in total awe of the people around me and more in awe of one of my heroes, the one and only 'Brian May' of Queen, I managed to pluck up the courage to ask him for his autograph and if I could have a photo of us posing together – of which he obliged without question, and Anita Dobson (his partner and actress) actually took the picture.

But something happened to me that day that was going to take myself and my running to another level, someone was going to 'unknowingly' encourage me to take on bigger and better challenges – that person was to be Actress 'Vicki Michelle'.

I stood in the huge function room of the Dorchester Hotel where the presentation was being held and suddenly found myself staring at the gorgeous Vicki Michelle and though she has starred in various different productions, Vicki Michelle was at the time famed for her role as Yvette in the BBC comedy 'ALLO, ALLO' about occupied France.

I was too scared to ask if I could have my photograph taken with her so Ann asked her instead, I felt my legs turn to jelly as Vicki put her arm around me and posed for the picture – I was even more surprised when she didn't rush me away, but instead started talking to me and asking why I was invited to the presentation.

I explained that I had ran in the London Marathon a few weeks previous and was invited as a thank you for my efforts.

"So what are you plans now?" asked Vicki Michelle. "What's your next marathon then?" she asked.

"Well, I don't think I will run anymore marathons, for I have proved that I can run a marathon so I don't have to prove myself anymore," I replied to the keen celebrity,

"So you're telling me that now you have trained so hard to become athletic enough to run a distance that many fear, you are just going to let it all go by retiring – just think of what you can go on to achieve and all the charities you can help by what you do, please think about how fit you are because of running and how you can maintain that fitness by continuing with your hobby – and think that there is a whole more you can achieve before you decide to call it a day," she explained with great sincerity.

I guess that Vicki Michelle had no idea what her words were going to do to me, or what she was going to inspire me to go onto achieve in the future, come to think of it, neither did I.

Well, I came away with my head spinning of the day's events – Brian May, Anita Dobson and a word of praise from Vicki Michelle – I had a tale to tell everyone back at work the next day and I couldn't wait to get back to work I can tell you.

The following months had seen me training as hard as ever and I was entering all the marathons I could – The Potteries marathon in Stoke on Trent, Manchester marathon and anywhere that there would be a marathon as I would travel far and wide to run in any long-distance race.

However, things came to a temporary halt in March of 1996 when I was called out to an alarm at the Somerfield store that I worked, on my way there at around 5 am on a chilly Sunday morning and down Sneyd Lane, a horse jumped a fence and landed on top of my car.

It smashed the front completely and part of the roof, I tried to swerve to avoid the 'thing' (as I couldn't make out what the object was at the time) that had hit my car from out of nowhere, but ended up hitting a lamp post and giving myself whiplash.

The whole ordeal was frightening as I first thought that I had knocked someone off their pushbike, which in turn put me in shock and I just sat in a smashed-up car shaking and staring at the roof of the car.

I was taken to hospital where it was confirmed that I had whiplash and damage to the ligaments in my left arm. I was treated for shock and spent seven weeks at home unable to do very little apart from wash and dress myself.

After a lengthy lay off from work, I returned and everyone was pleased to see me. And as I had been training for the London Marathon, my accident had given me too much of a lay off from my training, so I was thinking about not running in the 1996 London marathon but something happened that made me determined to run in my third London Marathon in a row, that event was the arson attack on Liam's special needs school (Old Hall Special Needs School).

The school was almost devastated with pupils' personal items being burnt too, some pupils had their own wheelchairs especially adapted to suit their individual needs, and they were totally ruined too, so I chose to run the London Marathon to help replace the items that were special to the pupils.

I decided to run in the London Marathon in fancy dress, as I knew I was not going to achieve a personal best time due to my accident, but I was asked by a work mate (Dave Newell) if I would wear a costume made by himself, and I agreed.

However, the costume was a huge cardboard replica of the yellow three wheeled van that was in the comedy series 'Only Fools and Horses'!

This made huge headlines in my local media with television and radio news programmes covering a story of my training with the 'Trotter's Van'.

At home, things were getting a little worrying with Ann as she was becoming argumentative towards me, if I paid her a compliment, she would ask what am I after – sex?

If I did any extra chores around the house, she would ask me if I were guilty of something. I just put it down to the fact that I had a social life with my running and she didn't – so when she asked if she could go to aerobics on Wednesdays at a friend's house in the Penn area of Wolverhampton, I agreed – though I was suspicious of why she would drive over half an hour to Penn to visit a friend that I had never met. I thought it best to let her do her thing and hopefully she would start be a bit more cheerful and not give me as much grief about my training for the London Marathon.

And eventually, the London Marathon was yet again upon us and I lined up with thousands of die-hard athletes – wearing a cardboard van!

The jokes came thick and fast as passers-by and spectators were jokingly calling out, "RODNEY YOU PLONKER." "DURING THE WAR" and other quotes from the only fools and horses comedy show.

This lasted the whole twenty-six miles of the marathon as crowds cheered my brave efforts of running with the heavy 'costume', it was heavy but the further I carried it, the heavier it became.

I reached the twenty-six-mile marker of the race and with only 385 yards to run, I was totally knackered by this time so when a voice asked, "Fancy a race to the finish line?"

I was tempted to say no, but when I turned to see a man in a 'Pot Noodle' costume I just couldn't refuse – so for the last three hundred and eighty yards of the London Marathon, I was in a two-man race with a 'Chicken and Mushroom POT NOODLE'!

It was a funny sight to see, a three-wheel reliant robin and a pot noodle sprinting past tired and weary runners along the mall and on to the finish line. A commentator who was entertaining the crowds along the mall started to give a running commentary of the race between us two costumed runners, "The trotters van has just edged into the lead…No, the pot noodle has taken back the lead…No it's the van…IT'S A TIE…A TIE LADIES AND GENTLEMAN."

The crowd of spectators just cheered and clapped at our performance, and in such bulky costumes we just bowed and waved to our new found fans and soaked up the admiration.

Back at home, though Ann was still being cold and nasty towards me, I knew that she was beginning to hate me – but I had done nothing wrong to make her hate me. I was a little suspicious of her going to aerobics with her friends (or was she meeting another man), but my suspicions became more concerning when on one Tuesday evening when I was running with Sneyd Striders and past the Somerfield store, I could see that our car wasn't in the car park. I returned home where Ann's mother (June) was babysitting for me. I told June of my fears that Ann may be having an affair with someone and had gone to see him instead of going to work, but June just told me not to jump to conclusions.

So when Ann came home from work that evening, I confronted her by asking why our car wasn't on the store car park, but she said that she parked it around the back of the store because she was scared of thugs scratching it when the store was closed from shoppers and they were still inside working. When I asked if anyone else parked their cars at the rear of the store, she confirmed that Martin, a warehouse worker also parked his car there.

I was now bemused by her actions because she wouldn't have anything to do with me, and for no apparent reason she kept saying that our marriage wouldn't last long the way we're going! One evening, she called me from work to tell me that a male colleague (Martin) needed a lift home and she had offered to take him home, luckily for me, June was in the house and she watched the kids while I ran all the way to the store.

The look on Ann's face changed when I walked up to her on the shop floor and said, "I'll drop you off at home then I'll take Martin home."

She had no choice but to agree, and when I dropped her off, I started on my way to taking Martin home, on the way to where he said he lived. I told him, "If you ask my wife to give you a lift again, I'll kill you."

"What's your problem?" he asked.

"My problem is you, I don't trust you and if you go near my wife or try anything on with her, I will kill you," I snapped at him.

But being his arrogant self he smirked back, "What's up, are you scared of her being with a real man?"

On that I screeched the car to a halt and jumped out and I raced around to the other side of the car to drag him outside, but Martin had got out himself anyway. "Please, Glyn I was only joking mate, honest," he begged as he put his hands out to stop me getting too close.

I just ran at him and planted a punch to his stomach which sent him reeling to the ground, as he lay there trying to grasp his breath, I leaned over him and said, "This is where you get out, you can walk from here."

Chapter Three
Goodbye, Little Angel

On the evenings that followed, I had my suspicions about what Ann was up to at work and when someone told me that Ann and Martin were the only ones to have parked their cars at the rear of the store at night (with no-one else parking there), my suspicions were raised even more and I planned on hiding behind the store to see for myself if anything was going on.

However, Ann's mother kept reminding me what would happen if Ann caught me spying on her, for if Ann wasn't carrying on with Martin then we would be finished and our marriage would be over if Ann thought I was accusing her of having an affair.

So on many occasions, I would be ready to walk out of my house and try to catch the two 'lovers' at it by spying on them but on those occasions, June would talk me out of it. But Ann was still keeping me at arm's length as if to be punishing me for something that I hadn't done, and her threats of our marriage coming to a sudden end became more frequent as if it were a cruel and sick game she was playing with me.

At home things came to a head when Ann asked if she could spend a whole weekend in Blackpool with her aerobics friends. I said no to her request as she was a wife, and more importantly, a mother and if she wanted a weekend break then we should go as a family. "But you have been away to London for weekends away when running the London Marathon with your running mates, so what's the difference?" she asked.

"Yes, but I had offered to take the whole family for a weekend away but you kept refusing to go," I said in my defence.

The argument went on for a few days and with each day the argument got more and more intense, until one day I agreed that she could go but only if I meet the friends she was going with, all she needed to do was to take me to her friend's house where she did her aerobics. Let me meet her friends and then I would agree to let her go away for the weekend.

Though she said that she would take me to meet her friends, it never happened and in turn she didn't go to Blackpool on whatever weekend that was planned – again this had me thinking that was she going away with her mates (that I had yet to meet) or was she planning a dirty weekend away with another man?

It was a Wednesday evening that Ann came home from her 'aerobics' being towed by the AA, the car had broken down and she had to wait for the recovery vehicle in a rough part of Willenhall at ten thirty in the evening of which she was so upset by.

Just before we went to bed she said, "It's a good job Martin was passing by and sat with me until the AA came to my rescue."

"You what?" I asked in a loud whisper as not to wake the kids. "Do you expect me to believe that Martin was just passing by in an area he doesn't live in and an area you don't go past," I quizzed.

But Ann was adamant that Martin was her hero and behaved like a gentleman until the AA man turned up. I didn't believe her but I said nothing as I could see that she was so upset by the experience, however I was in turmoil as the thought of her and Martin having an affair played on my mind and tortured me all the next day.

I couldn't stand it, I decided to go home for lunch and have it out with Ann, but when I went home in the hope of perhaps catching Ann with another man, I found Ann sitting on the garden swing with a mug of tea in one hand and a cigarette in the other and she was sobbing her heart out.

I made myself a cup of tea and watched Ann in the garden as I stirred my brew, she was sobbing her heart out and I thought that maybe she was ready to leave me but didn't know how to tell me.

Slowly, I walked up the garden to a surprised Ann, surprised to see me home from work. "What are you doing home?" she asked.

"More like what are you doing crying on the swing," I replied.

"Oh, I have had a huge bust up with my mum and I'm upset," she answered.

"Why are you getting upset after a row with your mother?" I laughed. "You and your mum are always falling out, you'll be talking to each other again tomorrow," I continued.

But Ann told me that the experience of the car breaking down, Liam's autism problems and arguing with June had all got on top of her and she felt the need to get it out of her system by having a good cry.

I didn't believe her and thought that maybe Martin was more of the reason she was upset than she was telling me.

It wasn't long after this that Martin left the company and on to a new job, and I supposed that I was relieved that the potential threat to my marriage was now out of the way and I could relax more and get on with my life, but the thought of Ann having an affair with Martin still haunted my mind and was to plague me for many years to come.

Ann had started to support me with my running now and came along to races to cheer me over the finish line of my marathons, it was great to see my family shouting out my name as I crossed the finish line, and to get hugs and kisses from my proud wife was adding to the magic of my running achievements. I felt like a good strong family unit again and my reputation was getting bigger as the local newspapers printed stories of my marathon achievements. I wasn't the only man in Willenhall to run in marathons but due to the fact that I had quit smoking and became a local hero and was running many miles for charity, I became a focus for local media – and I loved every minute of it!

Life was feeling a little better now and it seemed that I had got no worries in the world, until I got a phone call from my mum one Saturday evening.

"Glyn get to North Staffordshire hospital as soon as you can," she begged.

"But that's near Stoke on Trent," I replied.

"They've rushed Kate's youngest to hospital, they think she has meningitis," cried my mum. I drove all the way up the M6 motorway and wasn't too sure of where the hospital was but I eventually found it and parked the car anywhere I could; rushing into the hospital I ran up and down corridors looking for the ward that Alix Rae was in (Alix Rae being the name of Kate's daughter).

I stopped in my tracks as I came to a room which had a huge plate glass window at the front and a bed in the middle of the room, besides the bed was my sister and her boyfriend.

Kate and her partner were crying their eyes out as they looked over a huge purple baby that was laid on the bed, Alix Rae had contracted septicaemia from meningitis and looked like a huge plum.

On seeing me standing outside, Kate rushed to me and threw her arms around me.

"Glyn, Glyn why has this happened to me?" she sobbed. "The doctor says that if she lives, she will lose her fingers and toes due to the blood poisoning due to Septicaemia," sobbed my sister.

"She'll be okay, she'll pull through just you see," I told my sister, as I tried to give her some hope in her distraught situation and in a way, I was hoping to convince myself that Alix Rae would pull through too.

"If she's anything like her mother, she won't give in without a bloody good fight," I told Kate.

"I acted as fast as I could, I took her straight to the hospital without delay," explained Kate. But Kate didn't need to explain anything, as we all knew that she was a dedicated mother who would do anything to protect her kids, but I suppose any parent in this situation would always question themselves as to the fact of 'what ifs' and 'may bes'.

On this, a few more of our family had turned up (including my older sister, Yasmin) and we spent a long time just hugging each other and trying to fight back the tears, trying to stay strong for Kate.

I drove back home and just sobbed my heart out all the way home, for I knew that Alix Rae wasn't going to survive unless a miracle happened.

I drove back down the M6 motorway and through the watery vision that was caused by the tears in my eyes, I managed to drive safely along the motorway.

Isn't it strange that there always seems to be a song that pops in to your life at a time when the lyrics seem appropriate to the current situation and this was one of those moments, for I had a tape of the 'Mr Bad Guy' album by Freddie Mercury in the car stereo and as I pressed the play button the song that played was 'There must be more to life than this'. As I listened to the words my tears become heavier.

Freddie Mercury singing, "What good is life if in the end we all must die, there must be more to life than this," was too much to bear but I just had to listen to the whole song.

Feeling so withdrawn, I went to bed and Ann soon followed, I couldn't get to sleep and after hours of tossing and turning, I eventually nodded off – but was awoken at four o'clock by the phone ringing.

"You answer it Ann, I can't pick it up, I know what the call is," I cried as I jumped out of bed.

Ann picked up the phone and looked at me with tears in her eyes, "Hello Yasmin...Oh I am sorry, so sorry," she said.

"I knew it, she's died, she's dead," I sobbed as I sat on the edge of the bed.

"Okay I'll tell him...Yes, I will tell him, and send our sympathy to Kate," continued Ann. I went downstairs and made me a cup of tea, (ain't it funny how we British always resort to a good old cuppa in times of trouble). Ann came down to me and we sat in the kitchen, Ann was talking about how Alix wasn't suffering anymore and how I have to be strong in order to support Kate – but I wasn't listening, I just sipped my tea and sobbed my heart out.

Four o'clock on a Sunday morning and I was just sitting listening to Ann trying to help me make sense of all this trauma, but how can you make any sense of a loss of a child that was only sixteen months old – I mean why can't sex offenders and murderers die at an early age and the innocent ones (such as Alix Rae) live a long and happy life! I suppose only the good die young.

Chapter Four
London to Brighton

So as the family tried to face the devastation and emptiness that was left after losing a young member of the family, Kate was left to try and get on with her life and organise her baby's funeral which would never be an easy task.

I spent most of the next few days in a 'trance like state' as I tried to come to terms with the loss of a young niece, I tried to put on a smile at work but it never lasted long and the depressing feeling took over my mind.

Kate asked me to do her one big favour, and that was to carry Alix Rae's coffin into the church along with her boyfriend's (Gary) brother, that was one uncle from Alix's mother's family and an uncle from her dad's family. I knew that this would be difficult for me to do but I couldn't refuse her this request and I agreed to give her this support at Alix's funeral.

At this time, I had left Somerfield and was working as a delivery man for a local bakery, well my job title was 'Bread Van salesman' and I would deliver bread to shops in a 7.5 tonne van, and for the first time I was earning a real good wage, even though I had to start work at three o' clock in the morning for six mornings a week, the pay was well worth the early starts.

At the same time, I had my own problems to face and more importantly the funeral was upon me and my duty of carrying the coffin into church, on that day I went to Kate's house along with the rest of the family and friends.

Kate's neighbours had all turned out to pay their respects and lined the street to watch Alix Rae's final journey, the grass verge opposite Kate's house was filled with wreaths and looked like a sea of flowers and made a pretty sight to see.

I walked over to get a closer look amidst the sounds of sobbing and the mumbles of, "Why would any God allow this to happen?"

Everyone was showing mixed emotions, some were weepy while others were angry, as for me I was just in shock and was finding it hard to take in. Kate was just being brave and keeping herself together for the sake of her other children.

I walked into Kate's house and the room where Alix Rae was laid in her coffin.

"Are you sure that you can manage to carry her, brother?" she asked.

I looked at the tiny baby in the coffin who looked as if she was in a deep sleep and as I bent over to kiss the little girl on the forehead, I replied, "Yes I will be okay, I want to carry her on her last journey, I'll see it through."

Just then the undertakers came in and screwed the lid down on the tiny coffin. I looked at Kate and asked, "Do they have to screw the lid down? There's a little girl in there," I continued.

"It's okay Glyn," replied Kate, "It's fine, it's fine."

The drive to the church was a solemn affair as we passed streets of onlookers who lined the route to the church with their heads bowed down and some were even crying, it was so overwhelming and so touching to witness.

Myself and Alix's other uncle carried the tiny coffin into the church, and as we walked slowly from the hearse, we were watched by more onlookers who were lined around the churchyard walls, before we had even walked into the church we were in floods of tears – grown men and crying like babies.

We rested the coffin at the top of the church alter and sat down at the front of the aisle, we watched through glazed eyes (glazed from our tears) as Kate read a poem for Alix and Garry tried to pay a tribute to his daughter but broke down before he could finish his speech, by now the whole of the church were in tears and the vicar had taken over by reading out a few words of her own.

The funeral was then taken to a local crematorium and we entered the room to the song of 'wannabe' by the spice girls – it was Alix Rae's favourite song and it put a wee little smile on our faces as we pictured a young girl dancing to the song as Alix Rae did so many times. But it was the final time we would see Alix's coffin as it was taken along a conveyor belt and into an 'hole' in the wall, it was at this time when the whole building went quite with the silence being broken by my sister Kate crying, then everyone else were breaking into tears, all in unison.

"Goodbye my little angel," cried Kate as her voice could only manage a whisper under the strain of what was happening.

Outside the crematorium we all hugged each other as if to try and give ourselves some comfort but the reality was a little girl had gone – which begged the question, "Is there really a God, and if so, WHY DO THIS TO A FAMILY?"

My parents put on a wake at their pub and though I was never a big drinker, I certainly downed a few pints that afternoon, which in turn made me more emotional and my tears were falling like a waterfall. My training had now become more important to me as I realised that running was my only way of dealing with the issues in my life, so I was filling my time doing what I enjoyed – and while I was running, I could escape the reality of life and put my worries to the back of mind, but even so those worries would never go away! My training became more intense and made me focus on the positive things in my life, which in turn helped to forget the negativity surrounding me which included the thought of my wife (possibly) having an affair.

The early starts at work were taking its toll and being a bread man was never going to be an easy job, for every shop wanted their bread delivered as early as possible so it was a non-stop rushing and running around schedule that ruled my working day.

I did use the early finishes to my advantage and would run almost every afternoon despite feeling tired, this was my 'benefit' training, for if I could run on tired legs in training, I would run even better in races when I wasn't feeling fatigued.

The 1997 London Marathon had me running as 'Rupert the Bear' for muscular dystrophy, of which Rupert was their Mascot. God, it was hot in that furry costume but it was fun as the crowds were singing the 'Rupert the Bear' theme and little kids were cheering me on my way. I crossed the finish line and received yet another marathon medal and of course a hero's welcome when I returned home but by now, I was craving more from my running, for when I ran, I forgot my fears and my worries. However, I was fast becoming a local celebrity as my local newspaper featured many stories of my marathon running achievements, and the more publicity I got, the more I ran.

I had been invited to a try out for 'Gladiators TV' show and I was successful and completed the tough fitness test with flying colours. I ran on the treadmill (400 metres in under two minutes), followed by ten 'long arm' chin-ups, then traversed across a parallel ladder and climbing a 20-foot rope twice.

I was interviewed on camera which would be used on television (should I make it to the show). Unfortunately, I never made it to the final show but I had shown that I was fit enough to be a contestant on the show of which I was very proud. To go from smoker to a man fit enough to pass a physical fitness test for a television show was something to be highly proud of. By now, we had realised that Liam was falling behind his academic peers and he would fall even further behind as he got older. It was a worry for all the family but Liam was so loveable, and I don't think that I would have wanted him any other way but I was still worried about him.

So when I was running, I could escape my 'rut' and my fears for a while and be a real-life superman. Running with Sneyd Striders was great, as a group of adults would run and make fun out of each other for the whole of the training run, then finish off with pint in the bar after a hot shower. It was the support from Sneyd striders running club that spurred me on and on, for I loved every training session with the club and boy did we run some miles on club nights.

Toward the end of 1997, I was increasing my mileage and running anything between twenty-eight to thirty-two miles on most Sunday mornings. I enjoyed the gruelling regime that I had given myself and was focusing my thoughts toward running in an ultra-distance race (ultra-distance events being anything beyond a 26-mile marathon), and one event I had in mind was the 'London to Brighton', 55-mile road race – this was my goal for 1998, to run in my first official ultra-distance race.

By now, I had been running in so many marathons, and with each stride I took I was focused on the 'ultimate challenge' which was the London to Brighton road race – a 55-mile race and one of Britain's most prestigious ultra-distance events. The training became more intense and I had now increased the miles so much that I was running over forty miles on most Sunday's. The races that I took part in during 1998 were selected carefully as to give me some added training for my 55 miler. I would choose a marathon that was cross country and with lots of hills, my training also took me through 'Cannock Chase', a dense forest area near Walsall.

But the ultimate training session was a Sunday morning in September and a month before the race, where I ran from Willenhall to Cannock then onto Stafford, before heading homeward bound and through Rugeley – a Staggering forty-seven miles!

When I got home, I was totally gobsmacked – knackered, but gobsmacked, I slumped onto the bed and just lay there as my legs were as stiff as cardboard.

"How far have you ran today?" Ann asked.

"FORTY-SEVEN MILES," I bellowed out in full pride of my achievement.

"I'd better run you a bath then," muttered Ann as she couldn't believe how far I had ran – and why anyone would want to run that far anyway!

As I lay in the bath and let the hot water soak into my tired muscles, Ann proudly phoned all my mates to tell them what I had done, and the fact that I was well on course for a successful run on the London to Brighton. Ann had started to become a little more supportive toward myself now, and even though I was running more miles (and more hours) than before, she was doing less and less complaining, in fact she became supportive toward my quest to run in the London to Brighton race and even more so when I pledged to raise funds for Liam's school by running in the gruelling race.

All the neighbourhood were talking of this 'madman' who thought he was fit enough to run non-stop for fifty-five miles. People were wishing me luck and some were saying that I needed all the luck I could get as I would never be able to run for that distance.

But all the put downs and negative attitude toward myself just fuelled my determination to succeed and prove that I am fitter than anyone would give me credit for, so as you can imagine my training became more intensive and more punishing.

Work wasn't helping with my training schedule, and because I had to work six days a week, this meant that my Saturday training was done late in the afternoon instead of my preferred morning routine and as for Sunday mornings, well I had to run all of my training route feeling fatigued and weary!

For six days a week, I was getting up at 2:30 am, and though I would finish work at midday, I would go out for a run, making the most of Ann being at work (by now she had got herself a daytime job) and the kids being at school.

Though by teatime, I would always be flat out on the settee and fast asleep, but Ann would wake me up in time to get myself ready to go to the running club. Louise had become proud of her dad and went along on races with me to take part in the 'fun run' of each race, and how proud was I to see my little girl collecting her own medals from different races (though this stopped as soon as she reached her teens).

1998 was a strange year, for I was running more and more, but I began to think it was normal for a man of my age to go out and run twenty miles or more without even thinking about it, and I became a familiar sight in the community too and everyone would shout to me as I ran pass them. As for the 'Big Event' that lay before me, it was getting closer and closer and I was getting more and more excited as each day passed – but at the same time I was getting more and more nervous too.

However, news travels fast and I received a phone call from Central Television as they wanted to feature me on their news programme – Me on TV, BLOODY HELL!

Little did I know that this would be just one of many television appearances featuring my running and fund-raising attempts, myself and my support team were filmed on a training run and then interviewed in front of a huge camera.

"Tell the 'viewers' how you think you will do on the gruelling race."

"Well, my confidence is high and so I can't see any reason why I cannot be successful on the race," I stated. "Unless I get injured or something happens to put me off my pace and focus, I will finish the race in around eight and half hours," I stated with confidence.

Well, the whole neighbourhood had seen the news on television and I was the local celebrity, but with it came the pressure to succeed and return home with a medal, for there were still a small minority who thought that I couldn't do it – no way would I run for fifty-five miles non-stop, and if I could, will I be able to do it within the ten-hour time limit, so they were saying!

After spending the night in a plush London hotel, I awoke to find the day of the race was upon me and I hadn't slept a wink all night because of my nerves. I dragged myself to the race registration and collected my race number, then made my way to the start line which was on Westminster Bridge and in the shadow of Big Ben.

The crowd of runners had become more vast as the time wore on and straight away you could pick between the experienced runners and the novices like myself, for the experienced runners took their place at the front of the start line and the novices kept a low profile. "It's your first time then?" asked a runner.

"Yeah," I replied,

"I could tell," stated the runner.

"How?" I asked,

"Cos you're so nervous you're shaking like a leaf," laughed the runner. "Look a bit of advice, just run at a ten-minute mile pace, six mile an hour and that will give you a finishing time of nine hours and ten minutes. But of course take into consideration the hills and the fatigue you will get toward the final five miles and the time to stop to change any kit, and you should cross the finish line in around nine hours and thirty minutes," advised the runner.

"Great, that will be well within the ten-hour time limit," I thought to myself.

We all stood there waiting for Big Ben to strike seven o'clock which would signal the start of the race, and as the time got nearer to the top of the hour, the more nervous I became and the more 'butterflies' appeared in my stomach.

On a cool Sunday morning in October on Westminster Bridge, I stood and stared at Big Ben waiting in anticipation for the chimes to ring out 'seven o'clock', occasionally I glanced at my watch then glanced back at Big Ben until eventually, 'BONG' rang the bell to sound out seven o'clock; and as we all ran from Westminster Bridge, we could hear the remaining chimes ringing out in the distance which almost drowned out the cheers from the crowds of onlookers.

I had decided to run at a steady pace and keep myself focused on going the distance rather than trying to be a hero by becoming a front runner and risk 'blowing up' halfway through the race. I had the weight of expectancy on my shoulders for everyone back home was wishing me well because of the fact that I was running the gruelling event to raise cash for my son's school – Old Hall Special Needs School.

I ran for about three miles before my body felt relaxed enough to enjoy the race (if running for fifty-five miles could ever be relaxing), and then I came into my own and felt that I had the right to be in the event. I felt that I was going to be running across the finish line and no doubt about it! The atmosphere of the race was wonderful and as I passed a few support teams who were supporting other runners and I received a huge cheer, of course I smiled back and clapped my hands to acknowledge their encouragement toward me.

Then the same support teams (having seen to their runner) drove past some four miles further on and cheered me again, again I smiled back in appreciation of their encouragement.

And so before I had reached the twelve-mile point of this race, I had earned the nickname of 'Smiler' from support teams, marshalls, spectators and anyone who was following the race. I tackled the hills and the steep tarmac route in the best way I could, but with each mile that passed the more fatigued I became until eventually I was running the hills with a 'shuffle' as I barely had the strength to lift my feet off the ground.

But still, I kept smiling as I shuffled my way along the tough parts of the route, and still I was being cheered by what had become a fan club of mine.

"GO SMILER GO," came the cheers along the route and I just smiled back as I was too fatigued to reply. Just before I reached the fifty-mile point of the race, someone from the crowd of spectators called out, "The next mile or so you walk, don't try to run up the next hill."

And then when I ran around the next turning, I could see in front of me was a mountainous hill called 'Ditchling Beacon'!

"BLOODY HELL, HOW DO I GET UP THAT," I shouted to the crowds of support teams that were waiting for their runners to arrive.

But all I got in reply was, "COME ON SMILER, YOU CAN DO IT."

I walked up that steep hill, and in fact I passed a few runners who were actually trying to run up it themselves! The climb seemed to go on for ever and the gradient got steeper and steeper with every step I had taken, but eventually I reached the peak of the hill. I had reached the top of Ditchling Beacon and was cheered as I raised my arms in triumph and acknowledged that the final hill was behind me.

From the top of Ditchling Beacon, I could see the skyline of a town in the distance and that town was 'Brighton', just five miles was between me and success on this race and it was here that the aches and pains that I collected on the race began to ease.

A huge grin spread across my face as I ran toward the finish line that was somewhere on Brighton seafront. I became more faster as I got closer to Brighton and I was passing a lot of weary runners.

"Bloody hell, we still got someone smiling," shouted one race marshall to another, and yes with less than five miles to go I was so happy, so pleased with myself and the fact that a huge achievement was within my grasp.

I counted down the miles as I passed each mile marker, and as I passed each marker the faster my pace became until I turned onto Brighton seafront and the finish line was straight ahead of me.

As I sprinted the final yards to the finish line, the cheers of the crowd rang in my ears and the emotion of running such a gruelling route on such a long distance become too much and the tears started to well in my eyes. I crossed the finish line in a time of eight hours and twenty-eight minutes – over an hour faster than I had expected. As I was laid on a table and being given a leg massage, a crowd of people came over to me and hugged me and patted me on the back. "Well done smiler, you must be proud of yourself, well done," came the shouts of onlookers and well-wishers.

I had done myself and Old Hall School so very proud and the aches that came with running an ultra-distance race were nothing compared to the feeling of pride that came with finishing such a long-distance race.

Back home, the media were thrilled to be able to report the news of my success, and my local newspaper printed a story which bore the headline "HE DID IT" as for Central news, the report was the same as Michelle Robinson read, "Glyn Marston ran an incredible distance this weekend as he crossed the finish line of the fifty-five-mile London to Brighton race in an amazing time of eight hours and twenty-eight minutes, well done Glyn."

Everyone in Walsall knew my name and everyone at Sneyd Striders running club were so proud to have me as a member of their club. At work everyone was in awe of my achievement and the shops that I delivered bread to were asking me if I was that runner on the news.

It was great to be having my little bit of fame and I felt that I had earned it, for it's not every day that someone runs fifty-five miles in less than eight and a half hours.

Over the next eighteen months I was running in races of thirty miles, thirty-five miles or even forty miles and I was becoming a known name within the world of ultra-distance running (ultra-distance being anything beyond the twenty-six-mile marathon).

By now Asics UK had decided to contact me about the possibility of sponsoring me for my kit and I was never going to have to pay for any running gear ever again, and as my favourite running shoes were 'Asics Nimbus', this was a relief to have my shoes given to me on a regular basis.

I was to repay Asics by giving them a share in the publicity that all my ultra events generated and to be a guest runner in all Asics sponsored running events – I was to keep my fingers crossed in the hope that they will sponsor me. My hopes came true as I received an agreement for sponsorship from Asics UK – and boy was I over the moon.

I had now bought a new motorcycle, a Suzuki 500cc which I was to keep for a year then part exchanged for a Yamaha 600cc Fazer, and my new pastime became a reward for my tiring training regime, for when I wasn't running or working, I would go for a blast on my motorbike.

I was now craving even more from my running and was looking at running longer and further distances than any 'normal' athlete would consider. So when I heard of a '145-mile, nonstop running event' that started at Birmingham's Gas street basin and followed the towpath of the Grand Union Canal all the way to London's 'Little Venice' (near Paddington), I was more than interested.

I submitted my entry for the 145-mile Grand Union Canal Race (GUCR) in December 1999 with the thought of a new millennium and a new me, a super fit ultra-distance runner who had been given the nickname of 'Forest Gump' and so I had a huge reputation to live up to.

Chapter Five
The Grand Union Canal Race

The prospect of a 145-mile race from Birmingham to London was on my mind, and my every waking hour was focused on putting in the distance that would help me raise my game and give me success on Britain's longest annual running event that was a 145-mile non-stop running race – The Grand Union Canal race.

I was now working for Warburton's bakery where I was given a route that was in Tamworth and surrounding areas, and I loved the route and the people who I met while delivering bread to the shops in Tamworth, but training for a 145 mile was on the forefront of my mind – even at work!

So I would park my van a little further away from the stores that I was delivering to and run to the shop pushing a stack of bread in the hope that this gave me some 'resistance' training. With thirty-five shops to deliver to, this gave me a real hard work out for six days a week.

I still had a strict training regime after work too for I would run almost every day for ten miles or more and most of the time on my own too. I certainly came to understand what the loneliness of the long-distance runner was like while I was training for such a huge event, but it was something I had to do. Club nights at Sneyd Striders running club was surely better as I appreciated having someone to run with, though running with a group of runners was becoming difficult as the extra training was making me more fatigued than expected and I would have to dig in to keep up with my running club mates, especially on speed work.

Each day and evening I was out running no matter what the weather– rain, sleet or shine. I would be out pounding the streets and with each stride I took, I would be more and more focused on the race from Birmingham to London. On a Saturday, I would rest from my training as to give me a 'fresh pair of legs' for my long Sunday morning run, and boy would I run for miles and miles.

I became obsessed with the training and it took over my life as I bought a GPS watch which would tell me how far and how fast I had run (by logging onto satellites), and my running gear now incorporated all sorts of gadgets and hydration carriers that I could wear while I ran, and gave me the option of running for longer distances without getting dehydrated.

The London Marathon was soon upon me and as I had been training for a longer distance race, I should have no fear of a mere twenty-six-mile race. I had been running on most Sunday mornings for thirty mile or more in preparation for the Grand Union Canal race at the end of May. Publicity was getting bigger and bigger for myself on the Grand Union Canal race, and the pressure was on for me to fair well on the race and I was now studying the race in fine detail and setting myself a game plan for the great event. And so on Saturday morning on Whitsun Bank holiday weekend (May 2000), I took my place at Gas Street Basin at the start line of a long, long non-stop running race.

I had worked out a great plan for setting myself the correct pace and that was to stay behind 'Rod Palmer', for Rod was the only runner in the history of this race to break the course record for two years in a row, and so I assumed that if I was in front of this great runner, I would be running too fast.

The race organiser (Dick Kearn) shouted out words of encouragement then sounded a Klaxon to signal the start of the race, everyone set off in a conservative pace with some running just a little quicker than a walking pace and as for me, I was in the lead group and running alongside the more experienced ultra-distance runners.

By the time I had reached the ten-mile checkpoint at Catherine De Barnes Bridge, I was in the lead and still going strong, my dad (who would support up to halfway of this race) shook his head in disapproval as I ran through the checkpoint, but I thought he was shaking his head in amazement at my determination to not only finish the race but to hopefully win.

He was actually showing his concern for a son who was running far too fast too soon!

The Canal towpath was a little muddy and wet under foot as we came out of Birmingham, but the conditions was getting better and the towpaths drier as we ran towards Warwickshire. I was enjoying the views from the canal towpath and I became more interested in the scenery rather than concentrating on my pace and my game plan.

When I reached my dad and sisters at Hatton Locks, I decided to stop for a cup of tea from a flask that Yasmin had with her.

"Please slow down son," begged my dad. "You're running far too fast according to the race organiser," continued my dad.

"But I feel great, Dad," I smiled.

"You are on course for breaking the course record," pleaded my dad. "Which is proof enough that you are running too fast, please slow down," begged my dad once again.

But I was too concerned about the other runners that were passing through the checkpoint and I counted each runner as they faded in the distance.

I finished my cup of warm tea and set off on the towpath with determination to run past the runners who passed me while I was having a drink, and within a few miles I regained my place on the race – I was now in first place! As I carried on with full determination to be the 'hero' on this race, I received a call from my second support team to confirm that they had taken over and my family were heading home. They had arrived late at Hatton Locks and was now driving ahead in the hope of meeting somewhere on the race, unfortunately I was unable to tell them exactly where I was on the towpath and they were having trouble to determine where they were on the maps that I had given them.

I just ran and followed the towpath up to the thirty-five-mile checkpoint at Birdingbury Bridge, and by now the weather was getting hotter and hotter, so I was drinking more to keep myself hydrated. The sun reflected off the canal water, and at some points it looked like diamonds sparkling along the race but I was getting a little concerned about my support team as I was beginning to wish that I had waited for them instead of running ahead.

After reaching another checkpoint and filling my bottles up with water, I set off from there at a faster pace than I needed but I was focused on being the winner rather than just being a successful finisher on the event. I tried to call my support team but I had no signal and I was now worrying if I were to be successful on the race. I was running low on drinks but as I was in the lead on the race, I had no other runners (or support teams) to ask if they could give me some drinks.

Fifty miles along the towpath and I was completely out of drinks and feeling very dehydrated, panic started to set in as I wondered where they were or how far would I have to run before I would meet my team – if I would meet them before I passed out due to dehydration!

I called my two absent friends who were supposed to be supporting me and begged them to try to find me before I passed out, the response I got was they were waiting for me at Gayton Junction bridge, which was (according to my team) a further twelve miles away from my current position on the towpath, but in fact it was actually twenty-seven miles away.

That 'so called' twelve miles to my waiting friends seemed to be even longer than ever as the hot weather had now turned to rain (well it was six pm). My body was now shaking in my vest and shorts as my tongue was almost dragging along the towpath with my thirst making me feel light headed and dizzy, despite this I was still in the lead with the second-place runner almost two hours behind me.

As I reached my team, I passed out, only briefly, but I was not in a position to continue and so the decision to withdraw me from the race was made for my own safety.

I got home and as I walked through the front door, I stared at Ann as she told me not to be upset for at least I had a go.

The thought of failure on such an event was hard to swallow, and pride made me feel angry towards myself for running too fast for too long on the race. My dad shared his feelings on this too with words that I could not repeat but in the week that followed, I was to call the organiser to beg for another chance the following year.

And it was confirmed, I had another chance to take my place on the 145-mile race next year, and the next time I would get it right and hopefully I would get a dedicated support team too.

I went to Sneyd Striders running club on the following evening to tell them how I did, and with my head bowed down I explained to Trevor Simms (club chairman) that I was pulled out of the race at just past the 65-mile point of the race. On that, club captain Stan Harrison came to offer his congratulations.

"Sixty-five-mile, sixty-five mile non-stop. How on earth can you be disappointed of that?" Stan asked.

"Yeah," said Trevor. "You did yourself proud mate and you did the club proud too," he went on. I explained what had happened and the fact that I could have done better if I had the right support team, and on that Trevor Simms announced that the running club will be my support team on the next year's Grand Union Canal race, and support me for the whole 145 miles of the Birmingham to London race.

In all of the hassle of training for an ultra-distance race and trying to do my duty as a husband and father, I had forgotten about an event that I had applied for – to run the race of a lifetime! I had sent my running CV into 'Running Fitness' magazine in the hope of being chosen to run across the Grand Canyon, the opportunity to run 'Rim to Rim' that's to run from the North Rim of the Canyon to the South Rim.

I received a phone call one Friday evening in November from a man named Mr Paul Larkins. "Hello, can I speak to Glyn Marston," said the voice on the phone,

"Speaking," I replied.

"Hi, it's Paul Larkins of Running Fitness," replied the man on the phone.

"Congratulations, you have been chosen to run across the Grand Canyon," continued Paul.

I just paused for a while as I tried to take in what I was being told. "You mean that I have been selected to run from Rim to Rim of the Grand Canyon?" I asked as I tried to contain my joy.

"Sure thing matey," replied the editor!

After explaining the plans for the next few months – training weekends in the Lakes, VO2 max test on a treadmill at Loughborough University and publicity shoots for the Running Magazine, I hung up the phone and danced around the living room screaming, "YES, YES."

Ann looked at me and asked, "You're not really going to run the Grand Canyon, are you?"

"Bloody right I am," I laughed back as I couldn't believe my luck.

I was on a high and my running took on a whole new plain, I had to increase the level of training to help me through what was to be the most challenging races of my lifetime.

The Running Magazine had a test arranged for the runners of the Rim to Rim, Grand Canyon challenge which would see all six runners taking a VO2 Max test – running on a treadmill and breathing down a tube while having blood taken from a pin prick in your thumb, and it was at Loughborough University were I also met the other five runners and they were: 'Nick Janvier' a French runner who resided in Wales, 'Susan Preston' a young looking grandmother with amazing endurance from Kent, 'Duncan Beales' a runner with a great sense of humour, Louise Kisbee a young novice whom hadn't started running for long and 'Joanne Hicks' or Jo as she liked to be called.

We all seemed to get on with each other from the start and were really looking forward to the Grand Canyon challenge, however some bad news was to be given to me by Paul Larkins as he told us that the 'Rim to Rim' challenge across the Grand Canyon was to be taking place in May 2001.

For me, this would be clashing with the 145-mile Grand Union Canal race, and I had waited a year to prove myself on the race but I suppose that the Grand Union Canal race will be there for me to take on in 2002 and the Grand Canyon Challenge will only be offered to me for this one time only.

I pondered on the fact that I could take on both challenges in the same month, if my legs allowed that is, but some bad news was sweeping the nation and it came in the form of the 'foot and mouth' crisis, the media was full of stories whereas farmers were forced to have their cattle culled and could have gone out of business, losing everything they owned to the disease that was killing off animals in Britain.

I watched on television as farmers were crying as they struggled to face the reality of being financially ruined because of the foot and mouth disease, as for the countryside, everywhere was out of bounds to humans until further notice.

The crisis had the country in turmoil and carcasses were being burned on huge fires across the nation, but little did I realise that this would have a huge effect on my plans to run across the Grand Canyon and run in the Grand Union Canal race too.

As a lot of areas were out of bounds and so were a lot of canal towpaths too which forced Dick Kearn to re-arrange the 2001 Grand Union Canal race from May Whitsun bank holiday to the August bank holiday, for he could not have a canal race on which the runners would not be allowed to run along the towpath. And with the Grand Union Canal Race now being staged in August, I could take part in both the Grand Canyon event and the Canal Race.

I felt so terrible thinking that such a bad crisis were to be in favour of my running both the Grand Canyon challenge and the 145-mile race from Birmingham to London, but the truth was that with the canal race now being staged in August, I could now enter both events and have more time to put in the extra training for the Grand Union Canal Race too.

The local media was now full of a local hero running in a unique challenge. Local newspapers, radio and television were lining up to interview this Willenhall Superman as again I chose to take on the challenge to raise funds for 'Old Hall Special Needs School', the school attended by my son Liam and of which I was a parent governor. The local newspaper in Walsall (Express and Star) ran a great story of myself, and the photograph that accompanied the story featured myself and the pupils of the Old Hall School. Even the local television news (BBC Midlands Today) came along to the school to film the pupils at play and to film myself running (as if in training), followed by an interview by myself and Liam – and was he a star in that interview.

By now I had become even more known in the town than ever, strangers were coming up to me and patting me on the back – everyone was wishing me the very best of luck for the Grand Canyon Challenge, and I was feeling so proud of myself. Who would have thought that me, 'Glyn Marston', who was once told by teachers that he would never achieve anything in his life was now a local hero and a man who was inspiring others to take up a healthier lifestyle.

My life was fast becoming like an episode of a Rocky Balboa film, for everywhere I ran (be it on a race or in training), I was greeted with cheers and huge applause and cars would drive past me and sound their horns in admiration of this local hero. Everyone knew my name, knew all about me and my ego was fast becoming huge – well, if I allowed it to be, that is.

But for all the praise and cheers I got in running, I would somehow turn that into enthusiasm and this would make me run faster and harder than ever. I was now running for everyone in the area and not just for myself. My running club, my friends and family and my community were all proud of me now and I was not going to let them down by failing in any of my challenges – NO WAY.

My work was going so well now and all my customers in Tamworth had seen me on the news on the television, and therefore the sponsor money was coming in from the shops I delivered to. I delivered to a lot of co-op stores in Tamworth and every store was in awe of my running, and therefore every day I was treated like a celebrity, in all the surrounding areas of Tamworth – Glascote, Amington, Two Gates and the Town Centre. I was as well-known to the locals as I was in Walsall and Willenhall and I will admit to feeling so good about myself and boy was I enjoying being Glyn Marston, for my life was like a dream as I had everything I ever wanted – a wife and great kids, wonderful home, a good job and the love and the respect of my community.

Ann was now wrapped up in the admiration that I was getting from the community and she was so proud of her husband and his achievements. The same pride was felt by Sneyd Striders running club as all the members were telling stories of work mates and neighbours were asking about their runner by the name of Glyn Marston, more stories were being told to me of ordinary folk who were quitting smoking and taking up running – just like Glyn Marston, yes, I was an inspiration to my community and I was so proud of myself.

My training was now intense and because of the foot and mouth crisis, my usual Sunday morning run around Cannock Chase was out of bounds as the forest was sealed off from the public. My training regime was now a seven day a week affair with Saturday being a twenty-mile stint and Sunday mornings being a thirty-mile stint, and this allowed me to get used to running high mileage over a weekend – well, how can you train for a 145-mile race?

In the theory that you need to run a twenty-mile training run for a twenty-six-mile marathon, you would therefore need to run a 100-mile training run for the Canal Race, but 100 miles would not be a training run but a hard slog that would see you fatigued rather than fitter for the event. So, I planned my training regime to accommodate both hard training and recovery too, and it seemed to be working well. But as I was focusing on the Canal Race in August, I still had the Grand Canyon Challenge to take on too. But my Grand Union Canal Race training was still keeping my fitness in line with my Grand Canyon training too.

And as the Grand Canyon Challenge was getting nearer, the publicity for myself and the challenge was getting greater, especially in the Running Fitness magazine, for they were printing stories of the brave challengers (myself included) in every publication of the magazine.

This gave me a great sense of pride, and on any running event that I entered I was actually asked to autograph a few copies of the magazine – in which I would sign the pages that my photograph appeared on – I would reluctantly autograph the magazines because I never saw myself as someone famous, but the truth was that my name was becoming more and more well-known, and for all the right reasons too.

Now because of my new found fame, I was being the most photographed person in Walsall and this was noticed by a person who would be offering me something totally amazing.

For anyone who knew me would tell you that the only running shoes that I would wear would be a running shoes by 'Asics' and that shoe was called the 'Nimbus'.

It was once noted by Andrew Freeman (who just happened to be the Marketing manager of Asics UK) that every photograph taken of me or any filming of myself on television saw me with a pair of Asics Nimbus, and that was the reason for Mr Freeman offering me a sponsorship. I would be given all of my running kit and never have to buy any kit again.

With this sponsorship came a whole new publicity campaign and Asics UK had got my name in the national newspapers too. I was invited to Asics sponsored events and was now rubbing shoulders with television celebrities.

So as the time came near to the Grand Canyon 'Rim to Rim' Challenge, I was now carrying the thought of 'what if something wrong happens and I don't make it?'

With all the publicity I was having recently – local radio interviews, newspaper and television stories of myself and my running, I had a lot to live up to and this was added pressure for me. But I guess failure was never going to be an option for me on this challenge.

Now the whole point of the challenge was to run against a team of American athletes across the Grand Canyon, but we were told by Paul Larkins that the national parks in the USA had banned a race through the Grand Canyon and therefore the American team had withdrawn from the challenge! Now we were given the option of flying out to Arizona and having a week's holiday to the cost of Timberland who were sponsoring the challenge, but we as a team had other ideas, for we all agreed that if we weren't allowed to run across the Grand Canyon as a challenge then we could run in pairs and give the impression that we were just tourists rather than challengers. A great idea with one issue and the issue was that if anyone of us were to encounter any problems whilst in the canyon then we would have no back up in place and would have to finish the challenge no matter what!

So it was on – the challenge is still alive, and even though we were on our own as soon as we started the run, we still relished the thought of taking on the Rim-to-Rim challenge and the gruelling trek from the North Rim of the Grand Canyon to the South Rim.

So after a few hours of getting to know each other and some team bonding, we all retired to our rooms. Getting to sleep was a little difficult with all the excitement that was going through our minds, for me going to America was a real thrill for me let alone running across the Grand Canyon and as for Arizona – wow, I could not wait.

The morning was upon us and we took a short trip to Heathrow Airport. We all booked into our flight and then onto the departure lounge and were ready to board our flight. While we were waiting to board, we spent our time in the shops and as for me the 'gadget shop' was where I stayed for a long time until we were requested to board our flight.

We boarded our flight and the eight hours it took to arrive in the USA seemed an eternity, as I was a little less patient than usually, but we finally reached our destination – Chicago Airport, and my head was buzzing with excitement and the anticipation of the challenge ahead, it added to the thrill.

Chapter Six
A Grand Year

The time had finally come where we arrived in Chicago and then waited for the flight to Phoenix, for me it was my first time to the USA. The change in climate was noticeable as soon as we landed, the heat and humidity was intense (thank goodness our hired cars had air conditioning). The first thing we did when we got our hotel was to jump in the swimming pool.

Among the excitement was a little bad news, the National Park Rangers had banned a 'race through the Canyon' on safety reasons (understandable), so we had a choice: visit parts of Arizona for photographs for the magazine, or run through the Grand Canyon but have no help and no assistance if things got bad. Once we ran down to the floor of the Canyon, we would have to get ourselves back up to the other side on our own, no matter how tired or ill we may be feeling, and we would have to carry our own water and emergency supplies.

It was a huge choice to make, but myself and the other five runners were united in the fact that we had all trained hard for this, so we would go ahead and do it, even though we would not be racing against an American team, it would be just us six British runners.

Now the team consisted of: Paul Larkins (running fitness editor), Phil (running fitness events manager), Angus (photographer), Sarah (fitness trainer and sports physiologist) and Sarah Cosgrove (events manager for Timberland).

And then there were the runners: Nick Janvier, Susan Preston, Jo Hicks, Duncan Beales, Louise Kisbee and my good self.

We were introduced to a great man by the name of Dan Zeroski, for Dan had taken on this challenge a few times and had shown us the scars to prove it – 'SCARS'?

Oh yeah, it was at this point that we were told that we could be bitten by rattle snakes or stung by scorpions while running into the Grand Canyon, and the scars on Dan's legs was where he had cut the wound and sucked the venom out of his legs.

And so Dan was to run behind us all and be there for us, should we need to be treated for bites and stings. "I hope I don't get bit on the arse then," I laughed, "because I'm not having any man sucking on my bloody bum cheeks!" But then again if it is a choice of dying from a sting or having your butt pierced with a knife, the knife would win every time.

And so we ran in pairs and took it in turns to set off at intervals, as not to give the impression that we were racing. And as we set off from the North Rim it was cold, very cold, but I stood there in a t-shirt and shorts, and though I was shivering in the cold wind, I knew too well that the temperature would soon change as soon as we got started.

And I was right, because within 10 minutes of starting off, the climate was getting warmer, so it wasn't very long before the others were changing into t-shirts and shorts too. The scenery was breath taking, there were plants like I had never seen before and the rock formations made the whole challenge seem more like a sightseeing tour than a test of endurance. I spent too much time taking photo's (well, I may never pass this way again).

The rest of the runners had their own ways of challenging this run, some were in front in the hope of getting the challenge out of the way before it got too hot, and some who took their time as to keep refreshed for as long as possible. As for me, despite carrying our own emergency supplies (water etc.), I was too busy snapping away with my camera.

The whole challenge was amazing and as for the downhill run from the North Rim, it was supposed to be so easy, but the pressure of running down a constant slope for over an hour did take its toll on my knees but I was too busy looking at the beauty that surrounded me, for the views were amazing, so amazing.

A few runners took off ahead and as for myself and Duncan we just ran a little then stopped and posed for the camera a few times and we were really soaking up all this environment, for we had never been in such an amazing place before.

We finally reached the floor of the Grand Canyon and a place called 'Phantom Ranch' where backpackers and hikers could stay overnight before setting off for the second part of the Canyon (for only fools would try to complete a journey through the Canyon in one go – so we were told). After refilling our water bottles at Phantom Ranch, Duncan and I set off again for the second leg of the challenge and bound for the South Rim.

We reached the bridge at the Colorado River but then there was the sting in the tail – the uphill climb to the south rim. By now the climate had got hotter and more humid, but the steep climb up to the South Rim was getting steeper by the mile and my legs were getting heavier and heavier, and despite wearing sun block, I still got burnt. My face felt so sore that I wondered if I was really doing this for enjoyment. I kept running out of water, but thankfully there were drinking water points along the way (they seemed to pop up at the right moment).

Duncan, being the strong athlete he was, stuck to the task and gritted his teeth and got on with the challenge, but at some point, he had to give in to the heat and sheltered under a rock. After making sure he was okay, I carried on and plodded along on my own.

This was now a point of digging in and gritting my teeth and just get it over and done with – the sooner the better. After running for what seemed an eternity, I could see a group of people at the peak of the steep climb, it was the team from Running Fitness Magazine – this was the sign that the challenge was almost over, and I found myself going into a sprint to the top of the peak and to the cheers from the rest of the team.

I soaked up the adulation from my team mates and got changed into some dry clothes and not long after, I found myself being sick – this was due to the heat and humidity. I felt so sick for a while but as soon as I got adequate fluid back in my body, I felt great.

Not long after I had recovered from my nausea, I heard that Louise was struggling with the heat too and though she had Dan alongside her she was feeling really ill, so I ran back into the Canyon for a couple of miles to help her out by taking her some water and some moral support to get her to finish.

As I ran back down into the Canyon, Duncan jogged past me and he was puzzled to see me running back down into the Canyon – he thought I was running back to the North Rim, until Nick explained to him that I went to help Louise.

Louise had been so brave in this challenge and she knew that she had to get to the South Rim regardless of what emotions she was experiencing at the time, and so I reached her after running four miles back into the Canyon at a place called Indian Garden, and it was then that I realised that I had to run the bloody four miles back up again!

Myself, Dan and Sarah encouraged Louise all the way to the top of the South Rim and Louise was given a huge round of applause, for the rest of the team had rounded up the sightseers at the top of the rim to crowd around and cheer Louise over the finish line, and boy did she deserve the applause for the heroic way she got through the challenge.

As for the challenge, it was over and if I could, I would have done it all over again…every gruelling step of the way had taken its toll on my whole body as I ached all over, but yes, I would have welcomed the chance to do it all again.

The rest of the week was spent driving out to different locations for photograph shoots and quite a lot of action shots, whereas we would run with Timberland gear on and with a beautiful setting as a backdrop. Running around cactus trees and sandy hills were a real buzz and some of the places we visited were wonderful – such as Scottsdale and Flagstaff was so amazing. We visited a few places that looked like a scene from a western movie with some cafe's and stores having 'saloon' doors like in the cowboy movies.

Whilst doing a photo shoot on some deserted land, one of the editorial team (Phil) had decided to drive the jeep and kick up a whole lot of dust by wheel spinning the car, but this had been witnessed by someone nearby who apparently owned the land. So this guy rode up to us on a Suzuki motorbike and asked, "What the hell are doing on my land?"

"Where does it say private land then mister?" I asked.

"Here's where it says private land," he replied, as he pointed to a rifle that was strapped to his motorbike. "AND IF YOU DON'T HURRY UP AND GET OFF, YOU WILL GET A TASTE OF IT," he snarled. As you may have guessed, we shot out of there straight away.

Oh well, the week was soon over and we were back at Phoenix Airport and homeward bound. I was so pleased to be home and to see my kids again and my kids were so glad to see their dad again too. Local media was pleased to see me return too and the follow up stories was in all of the local newspapers. Local radio and television were so full of my achievement of running across the Grand Canyon and let's face it, apart from the other five members of the team who else had ran across the Grand Canyon? Well, I had not heard of anyone else who had such an achievement of running across the most gruelling landmark in the world – had you?

So the buzz of running across the Grand Canyon was almost fading away and the reality of running in the 145 mile 'non-stop running' event that was the Grand Union Canal Race was taking over again. The thought of running non-stop from Birmingham to London was in the forefront of my mind and I could not afford to rest on the laurels of my achievements of the Grand Canyon Challenge, for I had to keep my mind focused on the race and to prove that I COULD DO IT. Everyone was now willing me to keep my training up to schedule and everyone at Sneyd Striders running club came out to train with me, and now my support team had grown into a military exercise (thanks to Nigel Churchill).

The plan was that I would run the first twenty-two miles on my own (this would take me to Hatton Locks in Warwickshire) with my support team meeting me at certain points of the route to give me drinks and food.

At Hatton Locks, I would be met with the first of a team of runners who would run ten miles with me and this would be the plan until I reach the finish line in London – yes, I was going to reach Little Venice and the finish line in London!

Britain was still in the grip of the 'foot and mouth' epidemic and though the crisis was getting less and less, there were still parts of the country that were out of bounds to the public – including the canal towpaths, however for myself it gave me an extra few month to recover from the Grand Canyon Challenge.

So instead of trying to run the 145 miles from Birmingham to London just a week after running the Grand Canyon Rim to Rim Challenge, I was given an extra twelve weeks to 'fine tune' my training. The weeks quickly passed and my days were taken up by delivering bread and running and then just sleeping, without the support and understanding of my family, I could not have got through my training. The August Bank Holiday weekend was upon us and I was all fired up for the Grand Union Canal Race, and this year I had a well-planned support team and even my wife Ann and her dad and his wife Jean turned out to support me.

It was a cool Saturday morning and I arrived at Birmingham's Gas street basin for the start of the 145-mile race, of course I was feeling nervous and the memories of the previous year was still in my mind.

But this year, I had a whole running club turning out to support me and they would not let me give up without giving it my best anyway. Nigel Churchill and Dick Johnson had planned the timetable of events – where they estimated I would be at certain points of the race and where I would meet my running 'buddy' at certain parts of the challenge.

Nigel took control of the support team along with Jill's husband, Steve Hill. He used his company's van as a support vehicle which was owned by Sean Haydon (a good mate of mine), and Steve was accompanied by Glyn who was Sean's cousin.

Another good friend of mine, a fellow member of Sneyd striders and a well-established triathlete who goes by the name of Simon Kimberley, was following me on his bike to give me moral support all the way to London. So everything was planned and all I needed to do now was run – 'All the way to London'!

With all my team telling me that I was looking great, I was feeling confident and ready to get started and I couldn't wait to take my place on the starting line in Gas Street, Birmingham. Gas Street was buzzing with the anticipation of runners talking about their game plan and the hopes of reaching the finish line at London's Little Venice.

I was treated like a celebrity at Gas Street because of my series of stories in Running Fitness Magazine, starting with my training up to the actual Grand Canyon Challenge. Almost everyone came up to me to ask if I was the man who had ran the 'Rim to Rim Challenge' and though I tried to stay modest, I did have a huge grin on my face as I soaked up the adulation of being a little bit of a hero.

However, the hero was met with some great expectation, as many were saying that if I were able to run across the Grand Canyon in 110 degrees heat, then the towpath of the Grand Union Canal would be a walk in the park – so, the pressure was on my shoulders even before we had started the race. I nervously walked down the steps to the canal towpath and lined up with all the other runners, we all stood there with butterflies fluttering away frantically in our stomachs as we awaited the command to get started. As I stood, there was more of a nervous twitch than an attempt to keep hydrated, for the tension got tighter and tighter as the time was counting down to the start of this extreme foot race.

And so as Dick Kearns counted down to the start of the race, I puffed a few times in order to control the tension that was running through my body – 3, 2, 1 – GO!

We all set off but this time I ran at a steady pace and not at the pace I ran the previous year, within a few miles the group of runners had separated with myself and a few runners in the lead group of runners and over a mile between us and the next group of runners.

Simon Kimberley cycled alongside me to remind me to keep a good but steady pace and I took his advice to heart too. At the first ten-mile point of the towpath, I was met by Ann and her dad who shouted out words of encouragement to me. I grinned back and gave a wave but I couldn't speak, for I was feeling a little emotional – yes, just ten miles into the race and I was still feeling emotional, this was because I was touched by the fact that so many friends had turned out in support of me and my dream.

I was totally focused on my goal and was running with one thing in mind – THE FINISH LINE! My heart was pounding with every step I took and though the butterflies in my stomach had gone, the anticipation of running in such a grand event was still with me and would be with me for the whole distance.

The first fifteen miles of the towpath was muddy due to the fact that we had some rain in Birmingham through the week and parts of the towpath were sheltered by trees, and therefore the sun had not been able to dry the towpath. I was enjoying the race and the views that accompanied the route, and for anyone who wants to see the beauty that this country has to offer, then take a journey along the canals of Britain and be amazed. Nevertheless, I was still getting butterflies in my stomach and the nervous tension showed no signs of easing. "Will I make it," I muttered to myself, "Will I get myself to London and the achievement of finishing Britain's greatest challenge?"

I ran along the towpath and treated the early stages of the race as a 'warm up' rather than a race and I kept myself motivated by commenting to myself about the views of the surrounding areas from the canal, and so I ran along the towpath, up Shrewley tunnel and then onto Hatton Locks.

At Hatton, I was greeted by a huge cheer as my team was waiting for my arrival. I took a few minutes break to have a sit down with a cup of tea then a change of clothes before heading off with Geoff Farnell as my running buddy. Geoff carried a rucksack with a change of clothes (should I need them), food and drinks too. Geoff reminded me that the running club had come out to support me because of the man I am, and that man being a caring and thoughtful person who had given Sneyd Striders so much good publicity from his achievements.

And as we ran for about four miles, we were greeted by shouts of, "HELLO LADS," from an oncoming canal boat, for the vessel had four young women on board and all four were 'topless', bloody topless and wearing thongs!

Well, Geoff almost tripped up over his own tongue and as for me, I was doing my best to stay focused on the race. At this moment, Nigel had called me to ask how I was doing but instead of being greeted by a dedicated runner on a mission, he was greeted by the calls of these women teasing myself and Geoff.

"WHAT'S GOING ON?" shouted Nigel over the phone.

"Oh, it's just a few ladies…a few half naked ladies heading to Birmingham's Gas street basin," I replied.

"Well, carry on running in the opposite direction mate…or else," ordered Nigel.

This put all the tension of the race to the back of my mind and made me realise that I should try to enjoy the event and just reach the finish line no matter how long it takes, and so this was the plan. Mac Mills took over from Geoff, and being typical Mac, he just chatted away about members of the club past and present and before long this part of the race was over and it had passed so quickly. Jill Hill took her turn to run with me and was her usual happy self, with words of encouragement she helped the next ten miles pass with ease.

By now I had run past Braunston and I was on my way to Blissworth and over the Blissworth tunnel. Steve Budjoso had taken over as my running buddy but instead of being met by topless women, we were met with a downpour of rain and were chased by a bloody Jack Russell dog too. The mutt had jumped off a canal boat and swam to the canal bank and gave a chase for about half a mile, before realising that its owner was getting further away, anyway it made this part of the race a lot faster than we had planned at this stage of the route.

In the miles that I had ran, I had passed Gayton Junction and the point of where I had pulled out of the race on the previous year, and so now I was running in new territory and way beyond any distance that I had ever ran before.

I finally reached 'Stoke bruerne' and the sixty-seven-mile point of the race, and by now I was in a good position on the race and well within the first ten runners on the race too.

I was feeling good, and despite the rain that was constantly stopping and starting, I was feeling confident and being well cared for by my support team. Nigel and Steve utilised the fact that we had two support vans by being at the pre-arranged points of the course and at a few other points too, which was an added bonus for me as I was able to take on extra fuel (food and drink). By now, my team was joined by Running Fitness deputy editor, 'Andy Barber' who came out to see how I was doing and to feature myself in the next edition of the magazine.

Ann and my in-laws were a blessing too for they cooked some food for me, and as Ann knew me better than anyone else, she was able to predict how I was feeling at many points of the race – for if I were chatting then I was okay but if I were quiet then I was feeling fatigued and in need of attention. Saturday night was almost upon me and the warmth of an August day was turning into a chilling breezy evening. Andy Barber decided to head off home and was so inspired by the dedication of my support team that he vowed to turn my story of the Canal Race into a story of a great running club called SNEYD STRIDERS. At this point I decided on a change of clothing and a hot drink before setting off and running through the dark of night along the towpath.

Also at this point, Kevin Postins had taken over as my runner and as we were going through Milton Keynes we came up against a 'road block'! For someone had organised an event in a field that accompanied the towpath, but they had blocked off the towpath with huge metal containers that were the size of caravans, this worried me but it had Kevin totally annoyed.

Walking up to the perimeter fencing, Kevin called to a security guard to come over to us – of which he did.

"WHO THE HELL GAVE YOU PERMISSION TO BLOCK OFF THE TOWPATH?" shouted Kev.

"Errm, I will call my boss," replied the guard.

"Tell him to hurry up then, we are in a bloody race," growled the usually placid Kevin.

And soon after came a man with a smug grin on his face, "Can I help you?" he asked.

"Yes, you can," snapped Kevin. "Who gave you the right to block off the towpath, it's supposed to be a public right of way!"

"What's the problem?" the boss asked.

"The problem is that my mate is running in a 145-mile race and you are blocking his path," explained a mate who was now calming down.

"Well, if you want to continue, you can follow the fencing and then get back onto the towpath, it's about a mile and half extra," the boss told us.

"A MILE AND HALF EXTRA?" snapped Kevin. "He is running a 145-mile race and he is not running an inch further mate," snarled Kevin.

I was beginning to fear that all my plans would go wrong due to this hitch, because it does not take much to put an ultra-distance runner off his stride – or to put him in a negative frame of mind which could see any runner just say, "OH SOD IT, LET'S GO HOME!"

And at this point I was tired and aching all over so it would have been an easy option to say, "I QUIT," but Kevin was so determined in his argument to gain my access to the towpath that I just couldn't contemplate the thought of giving up. And after a few more minutes of arguing, the boss allowed us to go through the fencing and onto the towpath and so we were allowed to jog along the dark, cold towpath until we reached the support team at Soulby Three locks.

It was Nigel who took over from Kevin as support runner and was running with me through the night, due to his military training he decided to run without a torch and therefore my night vision would be stronger, and if any of my competitors were in range behind me then they wouldn't be able to see me and would not challenge me for my position – and it worked too.

I kept a good strong pace with Nigel and the thought that no other runner had overtaken me kept me in a positive mood. Nigel just chatted on about his army life and the places he had been, he had a life that I once yearned for – a military life that was denied me because of epilepsy.

As Nigel chatted, I had come to the point where my body and mind went into 'auto-pilot' and my legs kept running but my eyes kept closing. I fought the feeling of tiredness by slapping myself in the face and then Nigel joined in...'SMACK' came the slap from Nigel's huge hand, along with a shout of, "Stay awake, you're in a race!" So I ran through the night and all I could see was the glow of street lamps in the distance from the towns that we were running through and all I could think of was 'the lucky sods, all tucked up in bed!'

I was feeling so tired and I was struggling to keep my eyes open but Nigel just kept talking to me; well, slapping me and shouting at times to keep me awake, and by 1 am I was sleep-running and as I ran, my eyes were struggling to stay open and I was staggering on the towpath and almost fell in the canal a few times but Nigel was there to pull me from the edge of the canal. Nigel was in form and pushed me all the way of his ten-mile stint with me, before allowing Ian Hill to take over for the next ten miles.

When we finally reached our support team at the end of Nigel's ten-mile stint, I was allowed a twenty-minute sleep... more of a power nap really, and after my nap and a quick cup of tea. I was soon on my way again, setting off toward the 100-mile check point that was less than seven miles away. The thought of reaching 100 miles was so uplifting as I realised that I was soon to reach a huge milestone on the race – and a huge milestone in my running career too.

As I reached the 100-mile checkpoint, I was greeted with a huge cheer from my support team and I soaked up the adulation. The 100-mile checkpoint passed with great ease, I continued along the towpath with the knowledge that the finish line was getting closer…okay, it was still forty-five miles away but to me this was so near to the end.

Stan Harrison ran with me when Ian's stint was finished, and as usual Stan was so encouraging and talked me into believing that I was a superhuman athlete, a real-life superman…and yes, I had left Clark Kent behind in Birmingham's Gas street basin and I had turned into superman from the first step of this race, according to Stan anyway. This part of the race had passed so quickly and I had passed five other competitors who were feeling so tired but the camaraderie between all competitors was great and even though it was a race, we still cheered each other along the towpath.

It was four o'clock in the morning and the tiredness that I was feeling was soon taken over by the feeling of my body waking up and feeling fresh again. At seven o'clock, I was given bacon sandwiches cooked by Ann and a wash by Nigel Churchill (top half only).

Ian Hill gave my legs the best massage that I had ever had which gave me the enthusiasm to get up and give Sunday and damn good blast and to reach Little Venice in good time.

The weather had been kind to me and my support team had been even better, for Stan Harrison, Trevor Simms, Dick Johnson, Colin Highfield, Ken Highfield and Dave Lockley all took it in turns to support me. And now, I was running with Trevor Simms who was so enthusiastic and pushed me to put in a strong effort as we closed in on the 120-mile stage of the race.

But it was on Trevor's stint with me that we were met with another hitch, for a builder's fencing was blocking the towpath and I was faced with the prospect of running back down the towpath and crossing the canal at a bridge some two miles down the canal and then running back up the other side of the canal, and therefore adding four miles to my distance.

Luckily for me, Trevor had other plans and tore down the fencing and allowed me to run on my way.

"There you go matey," bellowed Trevor, as I puffed in relief that I wasn't going to add more miles than necessary to this race.

But a few miles later, I was running with what felt a stone in my running shoe but as I took off my shoe, I discovered that it was actually a huge blister on my foot. This was hampering my running and needed to be gotten rid of, so I took a pin from my running number and pierced the blister, and I just ripped the whole blister from my foot.

This churned Trevor's stomach and he winced as I put on a blister plaster and then I was on my merry way.

The rest of the journey was met with great banter from my club mates, from Ann and my in-laws. I was fast approaching London and it was beginning to get dark, well it more dusk than dark and it was approaching nine o'clock in the evening. I was feeling so tired but was still very much focused on my goal to reach the finish of this great event. Nigel had decided to run the last ten miles and cross the finish line with me and so I continued along the towpath, and as darkness was falling the sweat was running all over my body and the smell of body odour was so horrid!

Finally, I could see a crowd of folk at Little Venice which was a sign that the finish line was insight. Dick Johnson ran out to meet myself with Nigel and Simon who had followed me on his bike and so all four of us ran together to the finish line.

Now with the disappointment of the previous year's effort, I was now full of emotion as the finish line got closer. As I approached the finish line, I could see Ann in tears as she gave in to her emotion and just wept with joy as I crossed the finish line.

Everyone knew just how much this meant to me, but not only had I finished the race but I finished in 'fourth place' with a time of 'thirty-seven hours and thirty-two minutes'. I gratefully accepted my finisher's medal and wore it with pride around my neck…and then burst into tears of joy, "I DONE IT…I BLOODY DONE IT," I cried as I waved my medal in the air.

A huge cheer rang all round as onlookers, well-wishers and support teams gave out a huge cheer in unison. Ann just held onto me and battled to keep her emotions under control as she sobbed. "Marston, I am bloody proud of you." Ann's dad and his wife just patted my back and shoulders in respect of a fantastic effort.

I acknowledged the fact that without such a great support team, I would not have made it halfway, let alone to the finish line, and therefore thanked my mates for their support as we walked to the support van. After getting changed into some dry clothes and put into a sleeping bag in the back of the van, I tried to soak in what I had just achieved, the distance, the terrain and the bloody weather too!

As my body began to relax, my muscles started to tighten up and every inch of my body was in pain – my legs were screaming in agony, my feet were sore (especially, where I had ripped off the blisters), under my arms were burning because of the friction from the rubbing of my running vest – yes, I had greased all moving parts including between my legs but I was still sore.

Quickly, I fell asleep as the rocking of the van helped me into my slumber and I slept all the way home and was carried into the house by a group of my friends and taken upstairs to the bathroom where Ann had run a bath for me. 1:30 am Sunday morning and I am soaking in the bath.

"Thanks for running me a bath," I spluttered to Ann,

"Why you thanking me for?" she replied. "I ain't letting you into bed smelling like that," she added as she sponged me all over with soap.

A few weeks after the race, I received the official results of the Canal Race and on reading them I noticed that another runner from Walsall had entered the race but quit after 40 miles. Now with it being common knowledge that I was running in this race, I got to thinking of why this runner had not approached me and asked for help in supporting him on the race too – well, it was his loss, I guess. Sneyd Striders had become more well known in Walsall because of the name 'Glyn Marston', and we were attracting more new members to the great club and a lot of female runners were joining our club too.

Chapter Seven
An Ambassador for Walsall

The name 'Glyn Marston' was well known to almost everyone in Walsall and everywhere I went I was asked if I was 'THAT RUNNING MAN WHO WAS IN THE NEWS', and boy was I soaking up the praise I was getting from the public. 2001 had seen me get awarded with 'Walsall Sports personality of the year' award, 'The Mayor of Walsall's fundraiser of the year' award. I was invited to numerous ceremonies as a guest speaker and asked to open Fete's – even present trophies to members of children's football teams.

I was now running in forty-mile races and 100k races (or sixty-two miles of running), even my training was now at a much higher mileage than before and with all this publicity came the adulation that ASICS UK were sponsoring me for my running gear.

Each time that I was featured in the news (either in the newspaper or on TV), I would be clearly seen to be wearing a pair of Asics running shoes…ASICS 'NIMBUS' RUNNING SHOES. The Nimbus were the only shoes I would run in and everyone who knew me, knew that the Nimbus were the only running shoes on my feet. Sneyd Striders running club were in awe of their celebrity runner, and every race that any member of the running club attended they were always asked – "Sneyd Striders, is that who Glyn Marston runs for?"

News was getting to me about ordinary people who had been so inspired by what I was achieving that they themselves had quit smoking and started running too. The attitude was if I could turn my life around and lead a healthier lifestyle, so could anyone.

And so with the thought that I was inspiring others to run, I was on a high which reflected in my running, for my training was taken on with great enthusiasm and everywhere I ran, I was greeted with shouts of encouragement or blasts of car horns to push me harder in my training. My local media were referring to Glyn Marston as an 'ambassador' to Walsall because of my achievements and the publicity I was getting for my running, and that publicity was now reaching further fields as sports magazines across Europe were asking for interviews or permission to write a feature about this modern-day hero.

So 2002 had started to become an eventful year but among the invites and interviews, I was still a family man with commitments and had to keep to a training regime for the Grand Union Canal Race and the gruelling 145 miles from Birmingham to London along an unforgiving towpath.

And so my usual routine was the London Marathon of which was now a training run for the Grand Union Canal Race. How strange it was for me to be undaunted by such a huge event as the London Marathon, but the whole London Marathon was a real buzz from the moment I collected my race number from the London Marathon exhibition on the Saturday morning to crossing the finish line on the Sunday.

And each time I ran in the London Marathon, I was raising money for charity and still getting recognised as the canal runner who ran across the Grand Canyon.

My family were supportive as ever which wasn't too easy with a son who was autistic, Louise had grown into a very thoughtful young girl and was totally understanding of Liam and his condition. She never got jealous of the attention that we gave Liam and I rewarded her with extra pocket money to make it up to her.

And so the Whitsun bank holiday weekend was upon me, and once again it meant running for the whole weekend from Birmingham to London on the Grand Union Canal Race – a whole 145 miles.

As the previous year, my support team was made up from the members of Sneyd Striders and as previously the enthusiasm was quite high from my mates but so was the expectation of myself completing the race in the top five finishers.

The plan was the same as the year before (well it worked well last year so why change it) and I would have a runner with me as a running buddy for ten-mile stints from Hatton Locks onwards. The weather had been appalling with a heavy downpour of rain in the days leading up to the race, but on Saturday the rain was torrential on parts of the race. I just kept on running as the rain bounced off my body and with my head buried on my chest, I carried on plodding along the towpath as I occasionally glanced up to view the path ahead.

I ran in the lead pack of runners, well on this race there were many runners whom would run behind in the hope of doing what I did, and therefore be in with a chance of finishing the distance.

The race had gone as well as expected and Saturday was ideal running weather, until the late afternoon when it rained heavily. However, the evening had soon fell and the rain eased a little but was still pouring on and off but my support team kept me focused on the challenge ahead of me – and kept me in good spirits too. Nigel Churchill had run twenty miles with me in wet and windy conditions too, but he didn't complain once and just kept me ticking along in a positive frame of mind.

The twenty miles had passed so quick with the fun we were having and (thanks to the torrential rain) the three hours that I was behind on last years' time was now reduced to one hour. Yes, I had made up so much time that I was only one hour behind my previous time at this part of the race, and therefore it made me more confident about finishing in a prominent place of the race. Dave Ireson was next to run with me as his stint started from the ninety-five-mile point of the race, and therefore he would have the honour of seeing me through the 100-mile check point. This was always a prominent point of the race for me due to my attitude of running beyond the 100 miles meant that I would not stop until I reached the finish line – well what's the point of reaching such a point of the race and then quitting?

Dave and I jogged up to the 100-mile checkpoint which was a huge tent in the gardens of the Grand Junction Arms Pub and we were offered a cup of tea of which we accepted gratefully. It was like liquid gold as I drank a hot cup of tea on a cold evening.

At the end of Dave's stint (and in the early hours of Sunday morning), I was surprised to be told by Steve Hill that the three hours that I was originally behind (compared to the previous years' time) was now thirty-six minutes ahead and I was looking at a personal best time, finishing faster than last years' time on the race and I was in sixth place.

So as I was sat down with a cup of tea (and Ian Hill massaging my legs), Steve showed me the times recorded at each checkpoint. "Look kid you are getting faster at each ten-mile stage and now you are past the 100-mile stage of the event…YOUR RACE IS ON MY SON!" Smirked Steve.

And by my team's estimation I was on target to finish the race in less than thirty-six hours, "BLOODY HELL MATE, YOU FINISHED LAST YEAR'S RACE IN FOURTH PLACE WITH A TIME OF THIRTY-SEVEN AND AN HALF HOURS, JUST THINK WHAT YOU CAN DO THIS TIME ROUND…THIRD PLACE," shouted an excited Nigel.

On that, I jumped to my feet and as I threw my plastic cup of tea in a bin bag I shouted, "OKAY LET'S DO IT."

Trevor Simms was with me on this ten-mile stint and he pushed me all the way. "Come on Marston, you have the pride of the club riding on your shoulders – do us proud mate," he encouraged.

Trevor handed me over to Stan Harrison at the end of his stint, now Stan didn't look like a finely tuned athlete but you try running alongside him, for he had a great pace over a long distance. By now, I ran through the dark of the night and was now enjoying the sunrise of a Sunday morning. I was also keeping myself motivated by thinking of the distance ahead being less and less with each step I took, and with myself running past towns and place such as Marsworth, Tring, Kings Langley and Watford, I could sense that the finish line was getting so near to me now.

Simon Kimberley had cycled the whole journey (and made a few pub stops along the way) and was now studying the race ahead, and though I thought I was in fifth place, I was actually unaware of a runner ahead whom had quit the race. Though he had reached 128 miles of the race, he was suffering so badly that he could not continue anymore which put me into fourth place.

Stan kept me in a steady but brisk pace and motivated enough to have some great confidence in my ability to cross the finish line in third place, and when Ian Hill took over as my running buddy for the next miles, I was on fire.

I reached the last checkpoint which was thirteen miles from the finish line and was surprised to be told that I was in fourth place, and the runner in third place was only a few miles ahead of me…and he was struggling to run due to his legs feeling so heavy and fatigue taken over his body.

And so onto the last time, my support team would meet me before the finish line, at Woodrow Bridge some ten miles from the end of the race, and boy was this an emotional meeting with my mates. I wasn't even thinking about stopping for a drink, well Steve Hill made me a cup of tea in a plastic cup and I drank it as I ran along the towpath.

There was one runner between me and third place on this event, for me to finish a place better than last year would be a great achievement, and so you can imagine I was running faster for the last ten miles than I was for the first ten miles of the race.

Eventually, I passed the other runner whom despite encouragement from his mates, just couldn't muster up the enthusiasm to race me to the finish line and he just patted me on the back as I ran past him (as a sign of respect for a fellow runner).

Nigel had run out to meet me on the towpath at less than four miles to the finish line, and so we ran with Ian Hill to the end. Those last four miles were the fastest and the most punishing of the race for me. Simon had cycled on to tell the crowd of onlookers of my expected arrival and had gathered a huge crowd for my finish. I ran and ran, with the view ahead of me getting more and more crowded which was a sign that the end was close. Nigel and Ian was now clapping as they ran with me, "WELL DONE MATE, WELL DONE," they shouted as they clapped whilst running along.

The finish line was well in my sights and a huge cheer filled my ears. I went into a sprint to the finish line and as the cheers got louder, the faster I ran.

I crossed the finish line to huge roar from the crowd, a third-place finish in a time of thirty-three hours and twenty-eight minutes – a personal best time of over four hours, over four hours faster than last years' time!

Again my support team had done me proud and without them I doubt that I would have made it halfway, let alone all the way to London. So, a tearful thank you from me to them was the first thing I did after collecting my finishers medal, and then the usual vomiting into a carrier bag before changing into some dry clothes and sleeping all the way home in the back of the support van.

2002 was to see me come into my own as an ultra-distance runner, and because of my high profile as a longer distance runner, I was now getting invites to take on greater challenges and one challenge was offered to myself of which I could not turn down – THE 24-HOUR TREADMILL RUNNING WORLD RECORD!

Well, in fact I was to take on the 100 mile and the 24-hour world record for treadmill running at Bluewater shopping mall in Kent, but this was to be sponsored by Reebok of which I was to be running in Reebok gear – including Reebok running shoes (and for a runner whom was well known for running in only Asics 'NIMBUS' shoes, this may have been a little awkward). To my delight, Andrew Freeman gave me his blessing and permission on behalf of Asics UK to run in the challenge and so my training was increased to make me fitter, stronger and more determined to blow this challenge and both world records apart.

So, June 2002 and I was making my way to Bluewater in Kent. I did want to take my motorbike and cycle the whole way but Ann was worried that I could have an accident, so I took a coach ride to London and then onto Bluewater.

After booking into a Premier Hotel that was paid for me, I just crashed out on the bed and slept for a whole twelve hours (which was a good thing for I wasn't going to sleep again until 24 hours or more after I woke up the next morning).

The next morning was strange, for I was hungry but I could not eat much, my stomach was churning and turning over and over – this was a challenge. I would not be running against another runner but running against the clock…against time, and would I break the world records, who knows for all I could do was give it my best shot and give it my all.

I met a guy named Rod at the Reebok shop in Bluewater and got changed into the Reebok running clothes that they gave me. Though I do admit it, the running shoes were comfortable to run even if I say so myself, but they would not replace my Nimbus running shoes.

I was taken to an area in the mall to meet the team that would be looking after me for the next 24 hours, but when I reached my 'spot' in the mall my jaw dropped as I saw this huge stage with a treadmill on it that could only be described as something that resembled an American Wrestling Stage, for it had a huge metal rigging all around it with huge lights all over it – boy, was I going to be high profile for the next 24 hours.

Nervously, I took my place on the platform and posed for the press and local media in front of a huge crowd of onlookers who shouted out (in unison) the countdown to my starting on the challenge…3, 2, 1…BANG!

So, I was now officially a world record breaking athlete because win or fail on this challenge, the public were so full of praise of my bravery to attempt a 24-hour world record event.

I increased the speed of the treadmill to give myself enough pace to break the record but without tiring myself out too soon, and I just ran at that same pace throughout the first few hours with my support crew calling out my progress at 15-minute intervals, "YOU ARE RUNNING GREAT GLYN," came shouts from Rod.

"Keep it up matey," shouted Kevin (whom was an ex-army PE instructor and was asked by Reebok to be in charge of my well-being on the challenge).

After 12 hours of running on the treadmill, I went to the toilets (which were conveniently close to the stage) for the 4th time and I noticed that my urine was brown – a bad sign for any athlete, for this was a sign of dehydration but what could I do to prevent my body going into shut down? I had been taking on fluids on a regular basis, I had drunk water and energy drinks quite often throughout, so why would I be going into dehydration and how long could I run before keeling over?

Quickly, I ran back on the treadmill and got back into the pace to ensure that I would break both world records but a little over forty minutes later, I was feeling dizzy and fatigued. I stopped and ran to the toilets again and again, I checked my urine, this time it was the colour of treacle and so brown that it looked like I was passing sludge.

I walked back to the stage and jumped on the treadmill and set the speed of the treadmill but this time a little slower than I was running before.

"Something wrong?" Kevin asked. "Are you okay?"

"No mate, my urine is a very, very dark brown," I muttered back.

"Oh God, take on more fluids," replied Kevin.

"But the problem was not to do with what I had drank but more to do with my body overheating," I replied, "Can we get a fan or something?" I asked.

Kevin managed to find a fan from a nearby restaurant and quickly switched it on to full power, and boy did it feel good to have a cool breeze in my face. I was ready to crank up the speed of my treadmill when suddenly I went light headed and felt sick.

"QUICK GET ME A BUCKET – QUICK," I spluttered out to my support team.

I carried on running on the treadmill as I was vomiting into the bucket and I was now wondering if I would make the 24 hours, would there be a chance of recovery as I had done on the 145-mile Grand Union Canal Race.

"CUT THE LIGHTS, CUT THE LIGHTS," I screamed as I tried to control the vomiting.

"If we cut the power to the lights, we will cut the power to the treadmill too," shouted one of the support team.

"CUT THE POWER ANYWAY," shouted Kevin.

"NO WAY, DON'T YOU DARE STOP THIS TREADMILL, DON'T YOU DARE," I screamed at my support team.

"I AM IN CHARGE OF YOUR WELL-BEING ON THIS CHALLENGE, SO DO YOU THINK THAT I AM GOING TO STOP HERE AND WATCH YOU KILL YOURSELF," shouted Kevin.

"WELL, IF YOU CAN'T STAND HERE TO WATCH ME, THEN SOD OFF AND LEAVE ME TO IT," I shouted as I ran and vomited at the same time, and on that Kevin disappeared down the mall.

I was now running on pride for I had no energy and no stamina, everything that I had drank and eaten in order to keep my stamina and strength in top condition for this challenge was now projected in a plastic bucket, and like a car, you cannot run your body if the tank is empty but carrying on running I did.

After half an hour Kevin returned with a deal…

"Right Marston, what if you break the 100-mile world record and then stop, how does that grab you?"

It sounded a logical idea, for at least I would go home with one world record to my name, and as I was at the 83rd mile of the attempt, another 17 miles didn't seem too far to run.

But the last 17 miles were so difficult, as the fatigue was setting in and my body was shutting down dramatically. My eyes were rolling to the back of my head and then back to the front, as I struggled to stay focused on breaking the 100-mile record.

My legs were turning to jelly and I wobbled for the last two miles of the challenge, until Kevin slammed his hand on the stop button of the treadmill and shouted out, "YES, HE'S DONE IT, HE'S BROKEN THE 100-MILE WORLD TREADMILL RECORD, with a time of 19 hours and 12 seconds," to which a crowd of onlookers who were making their way to work in the mall screamed out with delight at my achievement. I stood there and raised my arms in triumph and soaked up the adulation before crashing to the floor and completely falling unconscious.

I woke up in a nearby hospital just as the paramedics wheeled me into accident and emergency, and after handing me over to a female doctor, I was wired up to a monitor and had needles and tubes stuck into my body.

"We are admitting you into the hospital Mr Marston," said the doctor.

"No, I am fine, just put me on a glucose drip for an hour and I'll be right as rain," I replied.

"You don't understand sir, all your vital signs have gone, your heart has enlarged and so have your kidneys. We are treating you as heart attack patient, you are staying here for a few days," explained the doctor.

"NO WAY, NO WAY," I shouted as I sat up in the bed, but Kevin and Rod tried to talk me into staying until the doctors had checked me over thoroughly, and eventually I agreed to let the hospital do their work.

As I was wheeled into a ward, Rod and Kevin phoned Ann and gave her the bad news and it devastated her totally, she broke down in tears as Rod tried to explain that I was okay but I had a huge scare and will be in hospital for a few days.

And it was no surprise that only after a few hours of being taken into a ward, I received a phone call from Ann and as a nurse wheeled a telephone on a trolley to my bed and passed me the receiver, all I could hear was a sobbing wife yelling.

"YOU MAD SOD," she screamed down the phone, "YOU STUPID SOD. YOU OF ALL PEOPLE KNOW WHEN TO STOP RUNNING, YOU WERE SPEWING

YOUR GUTS UP AND YOU DIDN'T STOP…YOU HAD TO KEEP ON RUNNING," she continued.

"Ann, I couldn't fail on this, not with all the publicity I had, blame it on pride but I had to break at least one record on the treadmill," I pleaded.

"PRIDE, BLOODY PRIDE. WHAT GOOD IS PRIDE WHEN YOU ARE IN A WOODEN BOX, WHAT GOOD ARE YOU TO YOUR KIDS WHEN YOU ARE SIX FOOT UNDER," she ranted. Then she continued sarcastically, "On your tombstone it will say: HERE LIES GLYN MARSTON. IT'S A SHAME HE DIED, LAID TO REST BUT WAS FULL OF PRIDE!"

And then she burst into tears and sobbed hysterically and on that I put the phone down and laid back on my bed.

The next morning, the female doctor who had admitted me to the hospital came to my bed with a male doctor, a senior doctor. They both looked at the monitors that surrounded my bed and the senior doctor quizzed, "Why is this man here, he is fine. What's going on here?"

"I don't understand this," replied the female doctor, "He was on the verge of a heart attack when I admitted him, all his vital signs were virtually zero, no signs at all. He was all but a dead man according to his results. I don't understand," replied a puzzled doctor.

It seemed that my body had quickly recovered and because of how fit I was, my body had gone back to normal in a quick time.

The doctor carried out a few more tests on my body before telling me that I was going home that day, and boy was I happy. The senior doctor explained that the hospital are used to dealing sick folk, and are not used to dealing with fit folk like myself and I had puzzled his colleagues with the speed of my recovery.

He then produced a copy of a local newspaper which was opened at a page that featured my treadmill story and he asked me to autograph it for him.

I eventually returned home, and the fact of facing Ann and boy did she give me the biggest rollocking ever.

"What if you had died, what would happen to me and the kids?" she ranted, in one of those quiet shouts as not to wake the kids. "You are not running another mile again, EVER," she demanded.

But I knew that she could never stop me from running and after a week of rest and a whole week of local media interest – that were printing stories of 'Walsall's Sporting Hero' who had put his town on the map by breaking a world record, I was back in my running gear and pounding the streets.

Chapter Eight
Run Paris to London

December the eight 2002 and my 40th birthday saw me shave off my moustache in a vain bid to keep my youth. Ann had organised a surprise for me, of which I guessed a surprise party. Well, it is the norm to throw a surprise bash for someone who has just gone forty years old, isn't it? Not for Ann, for she had arranged a meal out with a few friends and an envelope, an envelope that confirmed that I was going to be running in the New York Marathon next year.

It was always a dream of mine (as it is of any Marathon runners) to run in the New York Marathon, so you can guess how excited I was when my family presented me with a letter of confirmation for my entry into the 2003 New York event.

However, the presentation of this letter was on December the 8th 2002. My 40th Birthday party and I would have to wait eleven whole months until November the 5th 2003, before I could take part in the marathon. My family could not have given me the surprise for this year, as it would have been given me a month before my birthday and therefore spoiled the surprise.

Well, the eleven months that followed passed a little quicker than I had expected, that may have been down to the extensive training regime of a runner with a busy work schedule, and boy did I work hard in training and in my job.

But early February of 2003 came news of an event that caught my eye and my imagination, for it was a group of runners that were going to run in an event that they called, 'RUN PARIS TO LONDON', and as the name suggested they were to run from Paris to London in one week – well, in fact they were to be running in the Paris Marathon and then run all the way to London and then run in the London Marathon all in one week.

Well, as I was entered into the Paris Marathon and the London Marathon too, I asked if I could join the event of which I was accepted, and therefore a new adventure was looming.

I flew to Paris from Luton Airport and checked into arrivals with Easy Jet, and it was in departures that I bumped into Gareth Davies (a seasoned Triathlete) and the organiser of this great event. We flew to Charles de Gaulle Airport and onto the race registration before heading to Paris and to the office of 'SHOPARAMA', who were sponsoring the event.

We all met up for food and drink and then set off to Colombes where we would be staying for the night, and so after a good night chatting about the week ahead and looking at maps and plans, we all had a good night sleep and woke up ready to take on the Paris Marathon.

I was in awe of the sights around me when I reached the starting area in Paris – the Arc de Triomphe and the Chands Elysees and more – here I was running in the Capitol city of France and the beginning of an awesome challenge.

Myself and Steve Broadbent had made it clear that this event was (for us two) a training event for the Grand Union Canal Race, for Steve had entered the 145-mile race for the first time in his life and he wanted to do well. Steve couldn't wait to meet me on this challenge for he had heard of my reputation on the canal race and wanted to reach the same achievement as I had on the previous two years of running the race.

We all set off on the Paris Marathon – myself, Steve, Gareth, Tobie, Paul, Arrie, Thierry, Mickael and Cheesa, for most of us a gentle but brisk running pace was the plan as not to tire ourselves out for the running that was ahead of us throughout the week, some 270 miles. We all finished the marathon in a good time, as for me, I crossed the finish line in a time of just under four hours, which would have been disappointing for me but I did stop along the way to take photographs – especially of the Eiffel Tower.

And so, when we had all gathered together at the finish line, we ran another five miles to our accommodation in Colombes, accompanied by Sarah who cycled alongside us and snapped away for photographs for the event website. When we reached Colombes, we all gathered together for a group photograph with our 'Run Paris to London' banner.

The next day was soon upon us and we were all warming up for the thirty-mile run to Lavilletetre, which was in the middle of nowhere but would be a welcoming sight at the end of such a long run, especially after running over thirty-one miles the day before. So, we ran away from Paris and along the River Saine, and boy was it such a great event to be part of with such wonderful views and such great company too.

We all ran together but it wasn't long before the group were getting stretched with a long distance between the strong runners and the slower runners, and so we were stopping at intervals to regroup and to take on drink and food too. Well, in Thierry's case, he would light up a cigarette before heading off on his run!

We made good time in the pleasant warm weather that followed us along the French countryside, and I decided to run with Thierry towards the end of the day as he was falling behind and complaining of an injured leg. We reached the small village that was called Lavilletetre and stopped off at a school which was to be our accommodation for the evening, and by the time that Thierry and I had arrived the rest of the team had cooked a meal and had it ready on the table. We were shown to a small sports hall and given crash mats to sleep on and so after a shower in the school changing rooms we all 'crashed' out and went to sleep. Well, tried to get to sleep in between the village clock going 'GONG' on the hour, and so my sleeping routine for the night was, nodding off…nodding off…'BONG'…WIDE AWAKE!

And this went on all bloody night and so I was facing a twenty-six-mile run to Montroty with heavy eyes and a tired body, but hey if I didn't get any sleep, neither did the others – did they?

It seemed that I was the only one that was kept awake by the village clock, as the others managed to eventually get to sleep and wake up ready for day three of the challenge. After a small breakfast, we all gathered outside the school gates, ready to be officially sent on our way by the village mayor. However, a scruffy looking man walked by and shook our hands and was muttering away in French. I looked at the man and jokingly said to my team mates, "Is that the bloke from last of the summer wine...Compo?"

To which Gareth replied, "Glyn, that's the mayor who is setting us on our way."

"Errrmm, pleased to meet you sir," I said as I shook the mayor's hand in the hope that his English wasn't very good, and on that we all set off waving back at the villagers who were cheering and clapping as we disappeared into the distance.

As we were running, I had noticed a 'bad vibe' from Sarah, it was as if I had upset her in some way but I just ignored it for a while and carried on running alongside Steve whilst chatting about the Grand Union Canal Race. Now, Steve had come along to this challenge as a competitor but if he had not have been with us on the event, we would have got lost, for Steve had bought with him detailed maps of the route and of the region. Gareth was armed with printed off maps from route finder from his computer and was not very detailed, and so we would all stop and check Steve's map to make sure we were on the right road, and it was at one of these stops that I challenged Sarah.

"Is it something I have done?" I asked.

"Well, if you want to know Glyn, I noticed that you didn't help with dinner last night," she replied.

"Maybe that's because dinner was cooked and prepared by the time I got to base last night," I said in defence.

"Oh yeah, be the last one in and you don't have to cook at all, is that what you are planning for the week then?" sneered Sarah.

"Hang on a bit, I was only last because I ran the ten miles with Thierry because he was struggling, and anyway, why haven't you had a go at Thierry for not cooking last night too?" I stated as my voice got louder.

"Thierry was injured and told to rest but hey if you think that finishing last each day will excuse you from doing any chores, then think again," shouted Sarah.

"HANG ON, I AM NOT TRYING TO GET OUT OF ANY CHORES, AND—"

I was unable to finish my sentence because Tobie interrupted, "Hang on guys, let's not argue, we have all week to share the chores so let's just get on with the run," said Tobie as he stood between myself and Sarah.

As we set off toward Montroty, Steve caught up with me and eventually the rest of the group caught up with me, and the conversation between us all was that Sarah was out of order for saying what she did. Gareth promised to have a word with her but I just told him to let it drop and forget about it.

However, with just over ten miles to go until we reached our accommodation in Montroty, I set off into almost a sprint and with the rage that was still in my head following Sarah's argument, I was determined to reach Montroty first and start the cooking. I reached a nice country house in Montroty and a nice woman lead me into the kitchen, two other women had cooked a meal of spaghetti bolognese and all it needed was to be served up. After saying goodbye to the three women, I waited patiently for the others to arrive and made myself a cup of coffee – WHY IS IT THAT YOU CANNOT GET A CUP OF TEA IN FRANCE, I COULD NOT GET ANY TEA ANYWHERE! And so the others arrived and I stood in the doorway and shouted, "OIH, HURRY UP BEFORE IT GETS COLD."

They all came into the kitchen and was amazed that I had reached the house so soon that I was able to prepare a meal for them all. "And I am not washing up," I stated. "Not after slaving over a hot stove," I said as Sarah looked at me in an apologetic manner.

Well, all the others stated that it was the best spaghetti bolognese that they had ever had and I just sat on the settee looking smug and smirking at Sarah as she was forced to thank me for the meal (and apologise for her behaviour earlier in the day).

The next day, we had run to Pommerval with no real problems and as the day before, myself and Steve ran together and reached our destination long before the others, and this was met with a little dissatisfaction from Sarah and Gareth, for they accused us of turning the event into a canal race training session. I just ignored any comments from the two and got on with settling myself down for the evening.

Our accommodation in Pommerval was a village hall with no showers, but had toilets with sinks and reduced us to having a strip wash in cold water in the sink!

The village was the last stop before Dieppe and our ferry to England, and as for our South African runners (Tobie, Paul, Arrie, and Cheesa), they were all feeling the colder weather by now and commented that it was a sign that we were getting nearer to Britain. As for Thierry and Cheesa they were forced to rest for today as they were nursing an injury which had hampered their running for more than a day now, but the rest of us ran onto Dieppe and into a snow fall. The South African runners ran to the support van that had followed us and put on as much clothes as they could, for they had rarely seen snow and was scared that the sudden change in weather would cause muscle injury to their legs; myself and Steve just laughed.

We reached Dieppe and boarded the ferry and for the first time in five days, I was able to get a cup of tea, a cup of PG Tips. Well, in the small time it took to cross the channel, I had drunk four cups of tea and I was in heaven.

We reached Newhaven and ran for about five miles from the port to our accommodation at Telscombe which was an hikers lodge and where backpackers stayed, and it was here that the arguments started again, for Paul was forced to return home and take his support van with him, which meant we were short on support for the team. Gareth asked if Steve and I would like to run the remainder of the event alone and unsupported as we were the only runners strong enough to run ahead and be self-sufficient, to which we agreed.

So the next morning, Steve and I packed up our backpacks with food and drink and was about to set off when Sarah stormed out of the house and stood in front of us stating that if we went on alone, she would announce on the event website that we were disqualified and deemed not to have completed the challenge.

A big argument followed with myself ready to thump Gareth, if he was to announce that I didn't complete the journey. And now the whole of the group were involved in a huge heated debate, and the problem was that Steve and I had decided on a slightly different route to the designated route that Gareth had set out. Well, if we were to be running alone it was up to us to take what we knew would be a better road to take, but Sarah was in disagreement with this, and so Steve and I ran on but to the agreed route to Lingfield instead of our own plan of running to Horley and then Redhill.

Steve and I reached Lingfield and waited in a cafe for the others to arrive, and while we waited, we went over the past week events and the highs of running from Paris to London. Unknown to us, a man who was a local newspaper reporter was sitting on the next table and overheard us, to which he asked if he could meet us tomorrow for a photograph and an interview for the local press – we agreed. Saturday and day seven of the challenge, and by now the nine runners that started out on the event was now down to six because Cheesa, Thierry and Paul was forced to rest so that they could be recovered enough to run in the London Marathon.

We set off from Lingfield at nine o'clock in the morning and after a brief interview and a photograph with the local press, we were in good spirits. Sarah was trying hard to put the disagreement of the previous day behind us and was really in a happy mood, and I felt that perhaps the strain of nine complete strangers running hard for a week had taken its toll on us all, but now that the challenge was almost over, perhaps the mood was getting lighter.

As usual, I ran with Steve and we took the lead from the start, which meant within the first hour we were a few miles ahead the other runners. We ran toward Blackheath and the end of today's run. I was whisked away to the London Marathon exhibition to collect my race number and to take my place on the Asics stand to have publicity photographs taken with the cast of Emmerdale TV series whom were running for the Asics sponsored Tvtimes Leukaemia research marathon team, of whom I was raising funds for on my challenge (as I was a member of the Tvtimes marathon because of my sponsorship with Asics).

Day eight of the event and the London Marathon, we were all in excited anticipation of the twenty-six miles ahead and of how we would fare after running over two hundred miles in the week. I crossed the finish line in a time of just over four hours, a little slow for me but I was happy with my performance and as for Gareth, he pulled out of the marathon just after running five miles due to a sudden pain in his leg. And so only five of the nine starters had completed the whole challenge and I was one of those elite five.

The day that followed the challenge, I was invited to BBC West Midlands Radio for an interview about my run from Paris to London, of which I accepted readily, but on the way to the Birmingham Radio station I came off my motorbike as I tried to avoid a stray dog that was running on the dual carriageway on the A34 into Birmingham.

My 600cc Yamaha hit the ground hard with my right leg beneath the heavy engine and a long line of cars behind me skidded to a halt in a desperate attempt not to run over me. I was helped to my feet by a few passers-by and I got on my machine and carried onto the BBC Radio station. I did the interview in great pain from my right leg and headed home as soon as I could, only to find that my right ankle was severely swollen and I was in need of medical treatment.

My good friend and neighbour, Martin Carney rushed me to Walsall Manor Hospital where I was taken to x-ray and the good news was that I had not broken any bones but I had damaged my ligaments and had my right leg in plaster for three weeks, but the 145-mile Grand union canal race was in five weeks' time!

I was determined to carry on with taking part in the 145-mile canal race no matter what! My local media was getting so excited about myself, a runner who ran over 270 miles in the previous week with no ill effects and no blisters but with just over ten miles from my home. I had an accident that will see me in a plaster cast for three weeks.

I had no choice but to sit around for the whole three weeks and be completely lazy but I was still helping my support with plans for the canal race.

The race went as planned and I crossed the finish line in third place and a time of thirty-two hours and thirty minutes, a huge victory for an injured man whose right leg was heavily bandaged for the whole distance. I was getting praise from everyone in my community and I had been invited to the mayor's parlour as a thank you for promoting Walsall and for being a true ambassador to the region, but my best news was yet to come. I received an invite to attend THE ROYAL GARDEN PARTY at Buckingham palace.

I had received a letter informing me that I had been invited to Buckingham Palace for the queen's royal garden party, of course my wife could come too. It was an exciting day for both myself and Ann, I had the invite because of the charity fundraising I had done from my running – the reward for putting others first – and it was the perfect excuse for Ann to have a new dress. I drove to London (as car parking had been allocated for us), we were really thrilled to be invited, and as we made our way to Buckingham palace, we could see the crowds of sightseers gathering around the gates of Buckingham Palace to look at what was going on. Ann and I walked into the grounds and actually through the ground floor of Buckingham Palace and into the gardens of the palace.

The mass of people that were there was amazing, all were soaking in the atmosphere and clearly proud to be there at Buckingham palace, Ann being the person she is got talking to a member of staff, who was there to assist the guests while we waited for the appearance of Her Majesty.

He asked Ann why we had got an invite, she told him of my running and the fundraising I had done as a result of my running. He in turn started to write down what Ann was telling him. "Have you ever met her Majesty, the queen?" he asked.

"What? Me! Met the queen, no I haven't," I replied.

"Wait there, I'll be back in a minute," he said, then he disappeared into Buckingham Palace. Five minutes later, he returned and took us to a part of the garden where we stood in line with a few other guests. We were stood there for a few minutes when her Majesty, the queen appeared. She started talking to each person in the line one by one, when Ann whispered (quite nervously), "We're going to speak to the queen, we are going to speak to the QUEEN."

Her Majesty was getting closer and closer.

What will I say to her? I thought, just then The Lord Chamberlain came up to us and announced, "MR AND MRS MARSTON."

We were very nervous and her Majesty could see this, thus the way she led the conversation, "You are the long-distance runner?" the queen asked.

"I am, your Majesty," I replied.

"And what races do you take part in?" she asked.

"Oh, a little race called the Grand Union Canal Race, it's a race from Birmingham to London," I replied.

But before I could continue with my sentence Her Majesty asked, "That's quite a distance to run, do you run it in stages?"

I explained that the race was a non-stop running event for 145 miles, with no sleep or prolonged rest periods on the way. Her Majesty was amazed that anyone could have the stamina to take on such a challenge. I was so proud to be given such praise from the queen.

Then she turned to my wife Ann and asked, "What do you do when your husband's off running all this distance?"

"Oh, I stay at home to look after the children your Majesty," replied Ann

"So typical," replied the queen, then she reminded me that I was lucky to have such an understanding wife (of which, I did agree).

We were the envy of many guests who came up to us to congratulate us on such an achievement – actually talking to the queen, and of course, Ann was saying only my husband could engage Her Majesty into a conversation of RUNNING!

We left the palace at the end of the day, feeling so delighted that we were fortunate to meet and talk to the queen. Our only disappointment was that guests were not allowed to take cameras into the palace, so we had no picture of the great moment. We weren't allowed to take mobile phones with us too, so we practically sprinted to our car to phone everyone at home to tell them of our day.

I received a call from a reporter from our local newspaper (Express and Star), who was aware of our trip to London and our invite to The Royal Garden Party. "How did it go today, Glyn?" he asked. I was just bursting to tell him of the day, needless to say it was headline news in the newspaper the next day.

Chapter Nine
New York City, New York

2003 had been an eventful year and the best was yet to come – New York Marathon.

In the gaze of the public eye, I was always looking at new challenges and original tasks to take on and one sprang to mind – What if I were to run from the Eiffel Tower to Blackpool tower? I had already run from Paris to London and now needed to run the distance between London and Blackpool to discover a safe route for myself. And so, a friend by the name of Phil Middleton was at hand to drive alongside me for safety's sake. For the next few months to come, we plotted a route with the obvious choice being the A5 out of London and in to the Midlands with a detour to the A34 through Staffordshire and into Warrington, then on to Preston and eventually Blackpool. As training got under way, I was followed a few times by reporters from Running Magazines, whom were already interested in Glyn Marston and his ultra-distance achievements. Thanks to Asics UK, these magazines were full of updates of my training and my planned route for the whole challenge.

So during April 2004, I would be running from the Eiffel Tower, Paris on to the London Marathon and then from London to the Blackpool Tower. With my route finalised and a few more sports magazines printing my story, I was on a high and could not wait to take on this original challenge that I had called 'The tower-to-tower run', and all my training was there for runners worldwide to read about and with lots of photographs too.

But first, I had the New York Marathon to take on and I had waited for over eleven months for this race, and as the time got closer to the event, the more I got excited – just like a kid at Christmas.

My local media had made huge headlines about their running ambassador by the name of Glyn Marston, who would be running in the New York Marathon, and yet again I was in the spotlight for my running. However, this brought about a call of mercy from a teacher of a local special needs school and that call was for myself to run the New York Marathon as a fundraiser for Castle Special Needs School in Bloxwich.

Well, as my son was at a special needs school, I found it hard to refuse, but when I discovered that the school had in fact been broken into and the pupils computers had been stolen, I was more than keen to raise the cash to replace the items.

The Express and Star newspaper in the West Midlands were now featuring the story in a huge way for the more publicity I got, the more cash we could raise from myself running the New York Marathon – and it worked for offers were coming in thick and fast with messages of good luck and notes of disgust to the thugs who could steal from special needs kids.

This had now made my trip to New York even more worthwhile and even more inviting and the anticipation was building up in a huge way from now on – New York, here I come!

Even though I was making this journey alone, I was still excited by the thrill of visiting the BIG APPLE and to run in the most prolific marathon of all. I could not wait to board my flight. I flew from Manchester airport and when I checked in, the excitement was getting hard to contain, for I was walking around with a huge grin on my face, this grin got even bigger when I boarded the plane!

The flight was full of marathon runners and the excitement could be felt all around the plane as most passengers were talking about their training and their expectations for the race.

"I read in our local newspaper that Glyn Marston is running in the New York Marathon this year," came a shout from a passenger who knew that I was sitting behind him but he wasn't totally certain that I was Glyn Marston.

"He's sitting next to me," replied a passenger who was so happy to be seated next to a local hero.

"Hi ya, my name's Glyn too," smiled Glyn. "Glyn with one 'N' like you," he went on. Which reiterates my pet hate of folk who spell my name with two Ns, every Glyn I know has the same pet hate, and so did the Glyn sitting next to me.

"Pleased to meet you, GLYN with one N," I laughed. "Is it your first time in New York?" I asked.

"No mate, I have run in the New York Marathon loads of times, so if you want any tips of where to visit and where the best restaurants are, just ask," he said.

"For a minute there I thought you were going to ask me if I needed advice on running the marathon," I joked.

"Bloody hell mate, me advise you on how to run a marathon, NO WAY," he laughed.

After a long flight, we arrived at our hotel and checked with the tour operator guide of which room I was staying in, and as I was booked as a single person, I wanted to know who was I sharing the room with?

It is normal for runners on races abroad to book with a sports tour company as a 'Don't mind sharing a room with a stranger' policy, whereas we are all runners and had the one thing in common, and it is great way of getting to know new friends.

I reached my room on the 6th floor and just dropped onto one of the single beds and as I wondered as to whom I would be sharing a room with (and would she be blonde), I started to nod off to sleep. It wasn't long after when the door burst open and a six-foot man stood there and shouted, "Hi matey, I'm Steve."

I jumped to my feet and introduced myself and then was told to get myself changed, for Steve had met up with two other runners at the airport and they were meeting up in five minutes to go out for something to eat and of course a 'drink'.

We met up with the other two guys – David, a Scotsman and John a true cockney character – and we all got on so well that other people in our hotel thought we had been mates for years. We had some great laughs drinking in different bars and sightseeing around New York, we spent a little time shopping (well you can't go to New York and not shop).

I bought a few presents for the family which included a huge 'CHUCKIE', the ginger haired character from the Rugrats cartoon. Liam loved the Rugrats and I thought that this would make an ideal present for him, however I did look a bit stupid carrying a 3 ft red head doll in my arms all round New York, and got funny looks all the way back to my hotel.

On the Saturday morning there was a pre-marathon event called the 'Friendship run', and what a great idea to get thousands of runners to jog around Central Park for four miles as gesture of sportsmanship.

And so we went down for breakfast and sat in a restaurant full of British runners, it was so embarrassing when quite a few runners came over to my table and asked if I was Glyn Marston – "Are you the Glyn Marston who ran across the Grand Canyon, ran in a race of 145 miles non-stop and broke world records for treadmill running?" came the questions from many other runners. The truth was, Steve had told a few runners that he was sharing his room with a world treadmill record breaker and the runner who had ran across the Grand Canyon – and so he had given a few folk the heads up on who I was.

"Yes, I am," I replied as I tried to remain modest,

But I was asked to have my photograph taken with a few of these folk who were in awe that they had met me (and why I don't know for I was never any kind of celebrity), but I enjoyed the attention.

And so after we had finished breakfast, we were asked to follow a guide to Central Park and the friendship run. There were groups of runners coming out of almost every hotel carrying their nation's flag. Myself, Steve, David and John were proudly marching with a huge group of folk carrying a union jack flag until I walked up to a few American police officers and spotted a pretty blonde officer. "WOW! You look wonderful in your uniform young lady, can I have my photograph taken with you?" I asked.

She laughed and agreed instantly and while Steve focused on us with my camera, a male officer placed his police hat on my head. I stood there in between a male and a female police officer with a New York police hat on which showed the great hospitality of the folk in New York and as for me – a picture that I will treasure for a long time to come – this was to mark the start of a good day and an even better weekend, for the whole of Central Park was full of runners of all abilities and ages with a vibrant atmosphere ringing out everywhere.

However, the next day, Sunday morning and the excitement was building up as we made our way to the coaches that were going to take us to the Verrazano Bridge and the start line of the Marathon. My nerves were terrible or was it the excitement of actually being on my to the start of this magnificent race?

At the starting line (Staten Island), the crowds were buzzing and all were eager to get started. I noticed a celebrity, well I only noticed him because he had a few minders around him. The celebrity in question was 'P. Diddy' or Puff Daddy to older music fans. "You're not making your crew run with you, are you?" I asked.

"Yeah man, it's what I pay 'em for, if I run, they have to be with me all the way," Diddy replied. And true to his word, they ran every step of the way with him. I was more amazed that I had spoken to Puff Diddy or P. Daddy, whatever he was calling himself at the time.

I got to the start line a little later than I should have and instead of starting in the three hours 30 minutes expected finishing time zone, I was in fact in the five hours and 30 minutes zone.

The race got under way and the thought of running twenty-six miles wasn't even in my mind, just the thought that I was competing in the New York Marathon, what a thrill it was to be setting off with thousands of other athletes.

I did however want to catch up with the runners who had set off in the three hours and 30-minute zone and give myself a chance of a respectable finish time. The race took us through Brooklyn, I ran along the route with the huge crowd of runners and I soaked up the atmosphere and the roar of the crowds of onlookers who had lined the streets. I was still watching the time on my watch, as I was now running faster than planned in a bid to make up the time that I had lost from being in the wrong zone on the start line. But after ten miles into the race and as we were running through Williamsburg and onto Queens, I found myself reading traffic signs in my head but with an American accent – I don't know why but it seemed like a fun thing to do especially when I read a sign that read out 'WALK DON'T RUN'.

It took away any pressure I had to perform at my best, it was the best way to approach such a race – and that is to enjoy every inch of the course.

The thought of gaining any personal best time on the race wasn't in my mind as this was an event to savour. I may not run this marathon ever again and if that were to be the case, then I wanted to remember the event with fond memories and not with a 'never again' attitude.

After running through the Bronx and Harlem, I was soon approaching Central Park and nearing the finish line. At twenty-three miles, we were running in Central Park and the roar of the crowd was so deafening – in fact, for the last three miles it seemed that no one came up for air as they gave out one long and huge ROAR. I crossed the finish line in a time of three hours and 39 minutes, not one of my greatest finishing times but respectable in any case, and I felt like I could have run it again.

I walked back to my hotel with my medal proudly around my neck, passers-by were in awe of my achievement as they asked, "Have you ran the Marathon?" I proudly told these passers-by of my achievement and allowed them to have their photograph taken with me. It is an American 'way of life' to treat unsung heroes as real heroes and to unleash their feelings of pride toward anyone who had done something to proud of.

That evening myself, Steve, Dave and John went out for a drink in The Playwright bar in Broadway. A group of New York fire fighters entered the bar and straight away noticed that we were British. "Are you here for the Marathon?" they asked.

We all went into our stories of how and why we started running, and I told of my 145-mile events and my run across the Grand Canyon. It appeared that these guys were attending a colleague's birthday party in a function room that had been booked for the bash and we were invited to the function upstairs. We were treated like royalty and as I drank a little more than I was used to drinking, these men were telling us of the '9/11' disaster that had taken the lives of their friends and colleagues. They told us stories of heroism that I had never heard before. We were asked to visit the site of the Twin Towers and to see for ourselves the scale of devastation that was made. We left the party at 3 am and staggered back to our hotel, where I just slumped on top of my bed fully clothed and slept until about 9 am, well that was when Steve woke me up with a cup of tea. It was to be a special day for the four of us, as we wanted to visit the site to show our respect to our new friends from the previous evening, and more importantly to pay our respect to the folks who lost their lives on that fateful day.

We did as we promised the fire fighters on the previous evening and was surprised to actually see just how huge the area was. It didn't look this big on TV, I can tell you.

I never knew that there were three levels underground, such as a shopping mall and the underground tube too, and the total area of devastation was phenomenal, as I pondered on whether I could dare to imagine what horror had taken place at that time.

One fire fighter was on hand to tell the tale of that fateful day and what I heard left me glued to the spot as I hung onto his every word. "Imagine seeing an aeroplane crash into the one tower, then phoning your partner to tell them what had happened, then your partner hearing you scream that another aeroplane is heading straight for your office...then the phone going dead," said this emotional man.

I was close to tears as this proud fire fighter went on to tell us about his colleagues who were fighting to run up to the top of the towers as the survivors were running downstairs and to safety. Yes, while many were in fear of their lives and trying to get out of the buildings, these brave men were actually running into the danger in a bid to save as many lives as possible without any thought to their own safety. I may add and of course, many died on that day and left behind grieving families who could only wonder why – WHY WOULD ANY HUMAN INFLICT THIS ON OTHER HUMANS.

There were many stories of unselfishness and bravery beyond the call of duty by the brave fire fighters who were called to the rescue of the victims caught up in the devastation. It just left everyone asking the same question, how could any human being even contemplate creating such a disaster? The rest of the 'holiday' was spent sightseeing around New York and visiting a few bars too. I loved the lights of Broadway and the views from the Empire State Building, even shopping was a great joy as it helped to soak up the fast-paced atmosphere of a great city.

Eventually, the holiday was over and though I had the time of my life, I had missed my family and was looking forward to giving Liam his 'Rugrats' Chuckie doll.

It was great to be home and to flash off my New York Marathon medal which is now in a frame and will be treasured forever.

It was difficult to calm down from the buzz of being in New York and everyone was in awe of my running in the great event. Sneyd striders runners club were so proud of running and fundraising from the event and as for Castle School for special needs pupils, they invited me to the school for a thank you assembly (of which made me feel so humble and proud of my achievements).

December was upon us and so was my 41st birthday, and the celebrations were a little less exciting compared to the previous year, but then we were preparing for Christmas and with two children it was always a fun time of the year. Even though Louise was an older teenager, she always played along with the Santa Claus scenario for the benefit of Liam who because of his autism, still believed in Father Christmas.

2004 was a really busy year for me, for during April, I had planned to run from the Eiffel Tower in Paris and then run to Blackpool Tower whilst running in the London Marathon in between, and I was soon to discover that I will have to put the challenge on hold or to postpone it altogether. Then I had the 145-mile Grand Union Canal Race in May and a few treadmill world record attempts in the months of March and June to take on too.

However, there came the news that I had dreaded or welcomed? I was asked to postpone my Tower to Tower run due to the filming of a documentary by the BBC, and I was needed to be filmed on the London Marathon, and then there was the filming of my life at home and work for the week that followed the London Marathon. I was forced to agree or withdraw from the filming of the documentary.

The BBC were planning to feature myself in a documentary about exercising and what drives me to run as much as I do and I agreed to be a subject for the documentary. And so, I had to focus on the London Marathon and then the Grand Union Canal Race. I had to train hard to be at my best, for I was going to be on show for the whole nation to see.

A film crew were to follow me and my support team on the 145-mile canal race from Birmingham to London and film everything that happened on such a race and what drives a man to put himself through such pain and what motivates him enough to actually run that distance without stopping. I booked a week off work as to make myself available for filming in April.

And, so the London Marathon was quickly upon me, yet again, I was to meet a BBC Film crew at the start area of the event. As I was renting a house in Greenwich with my mates from Sneyd striders, it was agreed that we travel to London together and share the driving cost as well as the rent for the house.

I recall reading the huge news headlines about top model 'Nell McAndrew' running in this year's London Marathon, and as I finished work on the Friday afternoon (and was in a marathon mood – happy and bouncing around the depot), my supervisor asked me, "What time will you run the marathon in this time mate?"

To which I jokingly replied, "Whatever time Nell crosses the finish line. I will be right behind her." Friday evening was spent packing my running kit and some spare running gear in case I decided to wear something different.

Saturday morning and I waited for Dick and the others to pick me up, and after waving goodbye to the family we set off for the M6 and southbound for the M1.

We reached the house and all chose our bedrooms, with Nigel and Dick sharing a room with two single beds. Myself and Simon were sharing a room with bunk beds (Simon slept on the top bunk) and Ken shared a double bed with Ronnie.

We jumped on the tube and made our way to the London Expo to collect our marathon numbers and look at all the stands on exhibition. I, of course loaned my services to Asics by spending a few hours on their stands to give my expertise and advice on the correct running shoes to buy. After reaching our temporary home and pinning our numbers to our running vests (and sorting out what we would be wearing for the marathon the next day), we went out for a drink at a nearby pub – oh yes, we finely tuned athletes were having a pint the night before a big event (to be truthful we were drinking coke and nothing stronger).

I went to bed and woke up with a great feeling of excitement, for not only was I taking part in the biggest race in Britain but I was being interviewed for my part in a BBC documentary and I just couldn't wait to get to the start line.

I left the house a lot earlier than the others and walked up the road to shouts of, "Glyn, Glyn can we have your autograph," from my mates whom were now walking behind me and poking fun at my television interview.

I reached the start area in quick time and was taken to a fenced off part of the starting line, where I was interviewed by the film crew in front of the London Marathon start banner. I felt like a star as passers-by were looking over and thinking that I must be a celebrity or something. "Tell us about your expectations on this year's Grand Union Canal, Glyn," asked a researcher. "Oh and reply with the answer in the question please," continued the woman.

"Well, in four weeks' time, I will be taking my place on the Grand Union Canal Race which is a 145-mile race, non-stop running from Birmingham to London where I have a great reputation, for I have finished 4th on two occasions and a third place, and so my expectations on this year's race is to finish in first place. I owe it to myself, my family and most of all, I owe it to my mates at Sneyd striders running club for turning out to support me all the way, the whole 145 miles," I stated confidently.

Unknown to me a celebrity had overheard my interview, that celebrity was the gorgeous model 'Nell McAndrew' who was being interviewed because of who she was and because she was running in her first ever marathon.

"Wow, you are a real athlete, aren't you?" she said in total admiration.

"Well, I do bit of running," I joked modestly. "Errm…what time are you hoping to cross the finish line then?" I continued.

"I don't know, four, four and a half hours I guess," replied Nell.

"Haven't you got a pacer, someone to make sure you run at a proper pace?" I asked.

"Not really, unless you want to be my pacer?" she replied and to which I readily agreed.

I became Nell McAndrew's pace setter for the marathon and I also became the most envied man on the event too.

So many a true word spoke in jest, as I recalled the Friday afternoon when one of my work colleagues asked me what I thought of Nell McAndrew running her very first marathon. "Well, whatever time she crosses the finish line, I won't be far behind her," I joked to my colleague.

It was such a special day and one of the most memorable marathons that I had ever ran, so I had an extra spring in my step as we started off on the marathon, but it was around the Cutty Sark (six miles) that there was a huge sound of wolf whistles and I looked at Nell McAndrew and I joked, "Are they whistling at you or me?"

"I think it may be me," she laughed, and then she said, "We have run over six miles together and I don't know your name."

"Oh, I'm Glyn...Glyn Marston," I said as we shook hands. She replied, "And I'm—"

I interrupted with, "You need no introductions I'm sure." But as we chatted on the race, I still couldn't help thinking of my last day at work, the Friday afternoon when I told my mates that I would be crossing the finish line with Nell McAndrew – AND HERE I AM, PRACTICALLY PACING HER AROUND THE MARATHON – as I said, "Many a true word spoke in jest."

Back at home there was a huge buzz amongst my family and friends, for I was unaware that we had been picked up by the BBC cameras at different points of the marathon, but they had all been watching the TV at home, and were busy phoning each other with words of, "Have you seen who Glyn is running with?"

As we ran together, I told Nell of my ultra-distance running, and she found it hard to believe that anyone could run for almost 150 miles without stopping. She wanted to know how to contact me, in case she wanted the help of an ultra-runner for fundraising in the future. We had no pen and paper, so she suggested that I contact her and she would reply.

When the finish line was in sight, Nell had picked up the pace (and so had I), but the nearer we got to the finish line, the faster we were running, so fast in fact, that I was struggling to keep up with her. I recall shouting, "GO FOR IT GIRL, GO FOR IT," and she did, crossing the finish in three hours and 22 minutes. I was two seconds behind her, but something happened that showed Nell McAndrew as the true, wonderful person she is. As the marshalls were about to

111

escort her to the media tent for an interview, Nell looked at me and shouted, "Glyn, thank you, thank you very much." A kiss and a hug was my reward for pacing her on the marathon and she happily posed with me on my finishers photo.

I made my way back to the house that we were staying in and danced in the kitchen as I told my mates of my running 'buddy' on the marathon and they listened with envy.

It seemed that good news travels fast in Walsall, for on my way home (in the back of my friends car), I received a phone call, it was Jim Dunton from my local newspaper.

"Hi Glyn, had a good race today?" he asked. He knew only too well what my day had been like, for he had seen me on the TV with Nell McAndrew.

"Yeah mate, I paced Nell McAndrew on the marathon, the whole 26.2 miles, Nell McAndrew and Glyn Marston ran together," I told him.

So the next day, when I got a copy of our local newspaper there were the headlines: 'Glyn, pacemaker to the stars', what an accolade.

As for Nell McAndrew, she did keep in touch – a signed photo, a thank you card and a letter of admiration for the work I do is what I have received from Nell.

I was now getting calls from folk requesting my help for charity fundraising, for opening new shops and to present trophies at sporting events. I was in even more demand as a community champion and a local hero.

Chapter Ten
Almost a God?

The 145-mile Grand Union Canal Race was upon me, and this time I was to be filmed by the BBC for a documentary, but unfortunately Nigel Churchill and Steve Hill were unable to support me on this year's race. They were both away on holiday and so Rob Drew took charge of organising the support, which came with great pressure this year, for everything was being filmed by the BBC and there were no room for errors.

I was in great form for this race (as usual) and ran at a good paced from the start but when I reached my support team at 82 miles into the race, I collapsed with exhaustion and my support were now faced with the possibility of pulling me out of the race. I was now vomiting and my support team were frantically trying to get me recovered and back into the race.

I was now sitting on a grassy bank at 8 pm on a Saturday evening and feeling sorry for myself, as I watched other runners pass by and by now my third place in the event was lost.

I couldn't quit the race, not with a television crew filming me and so I was forced to get back on my feet and into the race, and so after losing thirty minutes, I had to try to get back into the race and back into pole position.

At the 100-mile check point, I was almost four hours behind the lead runner, and so I had a tough task ahead of me if I was going to attempt to win this race.

I spent most of Saturday evening trying to recover while I ran and by daybreak of Sunday, I was firing on all four cylinders, so much was the desire to win that despite a badly swollen right knee, I ran past seven of the eight runners whom were in front of me. As I passed them, they would just gasp in amazement at the speed of my pace in the latter part of the race, they were so fatigued that they just whispered, "Go for it Glyn…well run."

I found myself in second place with less than ten miles to go and I was closing in on the first-place runner who was so tired that he was walking and had been for a long time. Simon Kimberley had cycled ahead and then cycled back to give me the information that I needed, "GLYN YOU ARE JUST OVER THREE MILES BEHIND THE FIRST PLACE RUNNER. TAKE HIM MATE, TAKE HIS LEAD OFF HIM…COME ON," screamed Simon in excitement.

I took a deep breath and instead of stopping for a drink at my planned meeting with my support team at the Taylor Woodrow Bridge on the Paddington arm of the canal, I just carried on with the first-place trophy in my sights.

As I bit my lip in an attempt to ease the pain that I was feeling from my right knee, I just ran as fast and as hard as I could, until I saw a figure of a runner who was jogging at a slow pace and he looked as if he was on his last legs.

I sprinted closer and closer to him until I was only a few yards behind him.

"Are you in the big race?" the jogger asked as he turned to talk to me.

"Yes, I am," I replied as I realised that this man was out on a Sunday morning jog and had nothing to do with the race at all.

By now Colin Highfield, Ken Highfield and Simon Kimberley had caught me up and were to be running with me until I reached the finish line.

"Bloody Joggers," I cried. "I ran my legs off trying to catch that jogger up, only to realise that he isn't in the race," I yelled to my mates.

"Oh well, at least you have made up more distance on the lead runner," claimed Colin.

"Yeah, but I am totally knackered now, who in their right mind would sprint for over a mile after running 142 miles," I sighed as I tried to get myself focused again.

My legs were so heavy, my right knee so painful and my eyes so sore from the effects of trying to stay awake, but I had to keep my mind on the task ahead and I had to look good for the television cameras that had been at unmarked places on the canal towpath along the route.

I crossed the finish line in second place with a time of 32 hours and 30 minutes, less than 20 minutes behind the winner.

I was delighted, tired but delighted by finishing in second place (even though first place would have been better), and I was followed all the way by a television crew who were tired themselves (and they hadn't run an inch).

Apart from the television crew, my support team and crowds of spectators at the finish line, was a grey-haired man by the name of John Foden who came over to me and introduced himself.

After shaking my hand he asked, "Glyn, will you run in this year's Spartathlon for your nation?"

"The Spartathlon?" I replied. "Okay, I'll give it a go, sign me up," I continued.

"I already have," smirked John, "I already have."

So I had no time to rest, for I was planning to break the seven-day world record for running on a treadmill and now the 153-mile Spartathlon, and still my knee was causing me some pain.

I returned home as a hero as usual, and as usual I was featured in my local media with the headlines: 'OUR GLYN IN SECOND PLACE, BUT HE'S STILL NUMBER ONE IN WALSALL'.

And as I was requested by a charity to take part in an event, the news was now that Glyn Marston was taking on another world treadmill record attempt despite ending up in hospital on his last attempt for a Treadmill World Record, and so the tension was so high for this modern-day Forrest Gump. Since my near-death experience on my first treadmill world record challenge in Bluewater Kent, Reebok gave me the actual treadmill that I had broken the 100-mile record on – an expensive treadmill that I was using in training and to be used on my next world record attempt.

The seven-day treadmill event was soon upon me and I was there running for 15 hours a day, seven days of the week but by now, I had noticed that the swelling of my right knee was huge and causing me a lot of pain but I chose to ignore it.

However, through the course of the challenge, well three days into the world record attempt to be exact, my right knee was so swollen and painful that I was forced to run with a knee support for the remainder of the attempt.

Despite this hitch, I still managed to break the world record in the gaze of the public and in front of television cameras for our local news programmes. The cheers from the crowds of shoppers that surrounded my treadmill was so deafening that I could hardly hear the news reporter as she asked me how I felt to be a world record breaker yet again.

I answered with excitement and pride but also with the relief that my task was over and done with, but so badly swollen was my right knee that I was a little worried and I should have rested it for a few weeks. But I had the toughest challenge of my life to train for – the Spartathlon in Greece – so I had no time for rest as I continued my strict training regime.

The months that followed were met with mixed feelings as my friends at Sneyd Striders running club were advising me to cancel the Spartathlon due to my right knee, but I was too focused and excited about this event and more excited because I was running for Great Britain and representing my nation by being part of the British team that were running in the race. And so, withdrawing from the challenge was not an option. I trained with a knee support wrapped around my knee and I was now wearing the knee support at work too because of the strain of driving for long distances were also taking its toll on my knee too.

About the Spartathlon, in the beginning, as Greek Mythology tells it, in 490 BC, Pheidippides (an Athenian messenger) was sent by his generals, from Athens to Sparta to secure help for the reinforcement of the Athenian forces against the Asiatic incursion.

Pheidippides arrived in Sparta on the very next day of his departure from Athens, 36 hours later in fact.

Many years later, in 1982 to be precise, a British RAF wing commander by the name of John Foden (a lover of Greece and a student of Greek History), wondered if modern man could run the 256 kms from Athens to Sparta in 36 hours.

Thus, he and four other colleagues set off from Athens to run the distance to Sparta, finishing at the statue of King Leonidas some 36 hours later and a 'MAGNIFICENT EVENT' was born. It was today in 2004 that was my concern, and as my wife and I were flying out to Athens from Birmingham, thoughts of brave Paula Radcliffe and her agonising end in the Olympic marathon came flooding back to me, for it was the heat and terrain that paid her brave effort on the 26-mile run. I had to endure that for almost 153 miles NON-STOP.

As we booked into our hotel, the nervous anticipation became stronger and as I registered at the race HQ, those damn butterflies were break dancing in my stomach as my nerves were taking a strong hold on my body, but Ann kept reassuring me that at least I was having a go and whatever the outcome, I would still be her hero but she was unaware of the right knee problem. Runners from all over the world were present, some who had finished the gruelling run on many occasions and some who had tried many times but had not experienced the joy of reaching the finish line in Sparta.

The race was just a day away and I tried to look relaxed as if not to be bothered by the event, but as I tried to look undaunted my wife could see right through me and did her best to calm me on the eve of this race.

We had met John Foden who was the man who had started this great event many years ago and as my wife was worried about driving in Greece, John offered to take her in his car to Sparta before driving back onto the race course to show his support to the runners who would still be in the race.

The day before the race was spent chilling out in the roof top swimming pool of our hotel and admiring the views of Glyfada from the roof top garden and bar.

I went through the programme of events again and again, for the organisers had really put on a week of special programmes for all runners which ranged from meals out to special coach trips, and as runners were there from all over the world it was a great way to get to know each other and try to break down the language barrier.

So Thursday evening, I had packed all my running kit into the boxes that were allocated for different checkpoints along the way, these items were to be waiting for me at my preferred points of the race – my drinks bottles, my energy gels, extra running vests and t-shirts, and just in case an extra pair of running shoes.

I spent a few hours in my hotel room trying to plot what I would need and where on the race, this was usually done by my mates at Sneyd Striders, and boy did I need them now!

As I agonised over what to have and where to have it on, the race my nerves started to kick in even stronger and dare I imagine that I would reach the 72-mile checkpoint before the cut off time? (or even reach the final checkpoint before the finish line, which was 6 miles from the finish in Sparta).

After doing all my pre-race preparation, I went to bed but only managed to get about three hours sleep, for I had never felt like this before, never had I felt so worried about anything in my life – had I done the right training, had I done too much or not enough training?

The thoughts went through my head repeatedly as I tried to get to sleep but I did manage about three hours sleep in the end.

Friday morning, and boy was I nervous, so much so that I ate very little breakfast as I just wanted to get this over and done with and hopefully be successful. John Foden being the man that he is, inspired me to think that I will give it my best and John wished me success for he didn't want to wish me luck as he said, "A man like Glyn Marston doesn't need luck, so I wish you success." And his words helped eased the nerves, I slowly took my place on the coach that was taking us to the Acropolis and the start of this great journey.

As we made our way there, I still kept wondering if I had the strength and endurance to make the whole distance. At the start there was a massive crowd of people who were amazed at the athletes (or 'Spartathletes' as we were called on the race) who were taking part in the epic event.

There were television cameras and television presenters – with huge microphones that resembled big fluffy rats on a stick – who would walk up to you and just stick the microphone in your face and ask you questions about your expectations for the event. I gave a brief commentary about my training and my expectations on the race before heading off to the start line.

As I approached the start line, I noticed that the Japanese runners had their own television crew following them, for ultra-distance running is huge over Japan – as is the SPARTATHLON. My wife waved me on my way as the race began and we set off for Sparta, my plan was to do just enough to get me through this race within the time limit and so I was horrified to find that within the first mile I was in 'FIFTH PLACE'!

Easing back on my pace and remembering how I hit the wall on my very first Grand Union Canal Race, I allowed the lead runners to disappear into the distance and I ran at a sensible pace. However, at certain points of the race it was so easy to let yourself get carried away and run a little faster as cars would sound their horns in admiration and crowds of onlookers would cheer the 'brave' athletes on.

The more they cheered, the faster I would run and was getting carried away with the occasion of the event.

The first day was hot and humid but it was bearable to run in. I was just hoping to get the first day over with feeling as comfortable as I could and then I planned to run a little faster during the cool night air.

The course was surrounded by stunning views and lots of hills. One hill was to take us over the Corinth canal and at this point it was clear to see how strong the camaraderie was between all runners even though we were from different countries and it made this race even more special. I was helped to pace myself by the information boards at each checkpoint, these had the checkpoint number, the time the checkpoint closed, the distance to the next checkpoint and the time that the next checkpoint would be closing. So, I passed my time by estimating how long it would take me to reach the next checkpoint (silly I know), but it kept me confident and my knee was not showing any signs of causing me any problems at this point.

Now this race was one where runners would pass each other over and over again, so it was no surprise that I bumped into two British runners by the name of John and Jackson, and these two were great company on part of this race.

However, Jackson had felt the need to retire from the race after battling an injury for some distance now and John had now passed me on a huge hill of which I could see him in the distance but I couldn't catch up with him.

John was going well and I mean really well but I eventually caught up with him in a village, but only because a crowd of children were stopping us for our autographs.

These children had literally run-in front of us and thrusted pens in our hands shouting, "PLEASE, PLEASE." We felt really honoured at this point and it made us realise just how much respect this event commanded for all runners on the race, for we were all treated as celebrities.

So as the race passed on, myself and John ran together and we passed the time just chatting as we ran.

However, the hills got steeper and longer and we were forced to adopt a 'walk, run' attitude up the hills, and so the plan to run faster through the cool evening was thwarted by the climbs leading up to Mount Sangor.

As we approached the 100-mile checkpoint, we realised that we had to climb over 'Mount Sangor', a steep and rocky uphill struggle that seemed endless. However, the views from the top was well worth the climb and I say the view from the top, for it was early Saturday morning and the only light we had was from the moon that shone above us, but the lights in the distance from the towns and villages made a stunning Kaleidoscope of colours.

As the day was breaking, we were getting fed up with the food that was available to us, not the fault of the organisers, for they had put on a great choice of energy food and drinks but we were craving something different – any chance of a bag of chips.

The support from the checkpoints were fantastic and the marshalls couldn't do enough for us weary runners, but I was now finding it difficult to digest food and therefore I was becoming weaker than I should be and with over 60 miles still to go.

So I started to chomp on sugar cubes which disgusted some runners but it gave me enough fuel to energise my body and keep me in the race, very soon I was feeling better and able to eat normally again (if you can eat normally on a race of this magnitude).

Alas, John was not so fortunate, for he had been feeling unwell for quite a few miles and told me to carry on alone and he would catch me up if he could recover from his ailments.

From now on I was alone and I was trying to get my head around the fact that the King Leonidas statue was still forty miles away in Sparta and the finish of this gruelling race.

I managed to motivate myself by imagining my running club, Sneyd Striders, cheering me on from checkpoint to checkpoint, and I was running this for my town of Walsall and more importantly, I was running this for my nation.

I ran alone for quite some time before I realised that John had retired from the race, and as I ran, I would look behind me to see the long line of runners who were behind me but alas, there were quite a few runners ahead of me too.

The second day of this race (Saturday) had been quite as hot as the previous day and I had discarded my hat (to my regret and my wife's disgust). The heat and the sun were taking their effect as my face was red with sunburn and my body was so over heated. The officials at each checkpoint had now grown concerned for this British runner as they would run to me as I approached each checkpoint with a wet sponge and whack it in my face.

"Are you okay?" they would ask me.

"Fine, I am fine," I would reply in a faint gasp as I tried to catch my breath, but the medics on the race were so concerned that I would collapse with heat stroke, but as I was well within thirty minutes of the time limit, it proved that I was still in good health.

And by now I had paced myself to stay within the thirty minute 'cushion' that I had set myself and I was doing great until I hit yet another steep hill!

And so as I began to walk up this hill with legs that were screaming in pain, I began to feel the hurt of a right knee that was not yet fully recovered. As I began to think back to the seven-day world treadmill record in Birmingham and the beginning of this injury, a voice bellowed out to me, "GLYN GET THOSE LEGS UP, CARRY ON RUNNING…NOW!" ordered John Foden (the originator of this race and the Chairman of the British Spartathlon team), and so I gritted my teeth and dug in deep and hard to run all the way to the next check point.

At this checkpoint, John Foden pulled me to one side and sponged my reddened face with a huge towel that he had taken from the boot of his car and dunked into a bucket of water. "Glyn, you have to dig in mate and push hard all the way to the finish in Sparta," he explained. "Time is now against you, Glyn, and if you walk the 9 km to the top of this mountain, you will not reach the next checkpoint in time and you will be timed out of the race, game over mate," John went on.

I dared not tell him about my right knee, for he would have pulled me out of the race there and then and so I was now faced with the fact that I was so close to the final checkpoint which was six miles away from Sparta but being close to being timed of the event.

"NO WAY, NO WAY," I shouted as I jumped to my feet. "I haven't come this far just to fail in the final stages of this race," I declared, and so I was back on the road and running like a man on a mission. I ran all the way uphill and tackled the 9 km that this mountain had thrown at me but after that hill, there came another one which was about 5 km of uphill slog.

With about 20 miles to go, I was unaware of the line of runners behind getting smaller and smaller, due to the fact that by now many were either 'timed out' of the race or some had retired from the event due to extreme fatigue.

By now, I had lost all concept of time and reality and just plodded on with tunnel vision as all I could see was the tarmac road in front of me. It was at this point that John Foden who was parked in a layby called out to me, "GLYN, YOU ARE NOW THE LAST RUNNER IN THE RACE, PICK UP YOUR PACE SON, PICK UP YOUR PACE. JUST PULL SOMETHING OUT OF THE HAT, SOMEHOW," he screamed.

As for me, I didn't want to cross the finish line in last place, I was aware that 140 runners had started this race and only 70 would finish, and to be amongst those 70 finishers is a real achievement but I wanted to finish in style – I wasn't going to win but I didn't want last place either.

So with a final six miles to the end, I went into a near sprint as pride gave my body new found energy and as I passed weary runners who were walking to the finish line, they just clapped me on my way as they showed their admiration to a runner who had plucked up the courage to put in a brave final effort.

John Foden drove past me in his car and sounded his horn in delight as he shouted, "GO FOR IT GLYN, GO FOR IT!" I guess he couldn't see the look of discomfort in my face as I winced in pain with each step I ran.

I ran into Sparta with an escort of kids on mountain bikes ahead of me and a convoy of cars behind, and no car tried to overtake me and this was a mark of respect to a weary runner. I had run all the way with my club vest that bore the logo 'SNEYD STRIDERS, WALSALL' and my union jack shorts, and therefore I had become a prominent runner on the race and I had made a lot of friends and admirers along the way, so why wasn't I surprised to see a long line of well-wishers lining up the avenue to the statue of King Leonidas.

Cars blasted their horns and police sirens wailed as to inform the crowd at the finish of my approach, and as I ran, I could see the King Leonidas statue closing in ahead of me. As the cheers got louder, I began to run faster and by now there were locals leaning out of windows and shouting their respect to another runner who had shown the bravery to take on this challenge. My legs were screaming in pain and my right knee was now close to giving up but I managed to continue with my sprint as I ran up the few steps to the statue, and as I reached the top step, my right knee gave way for a split second but I was able to stay on my feet and just wobbled a little in front of a huge crowd that were cheering my success; with those cheers ringing in my ears, I kissed the foot of the statue as to signal that I had finished my race.

The cheers were deafening as I stood to soak up my applause and with two young Greek women dressed as goddesses handed me a drink of water from the Evrotas River (whilst the other placed an Olive wreath around my head), I caught the eye of my wife who was now crying tears of joy for her husband.

Everyone who knew me would know what this race meant to me, and as I realised the sense of my achievement, I too started to feel tears rolling down my cheeks.

I had not won this race, nor had I broken any records on the event too, but to run 153 miles non-stop was gruelling enough. To endure the mountains and constant uphills whilst running in this heat and humidity was even more impressive.

As I soaked up the adulation of successfully finishing the race, I was being ushered to a huge marquee, a medical tent where I was sat down and had two nurses massage my legs as my feet were allowed to soak in warm disinfected water. "Ooh that feels good," I gently moaned as my wife stood at the doorway and stared as I was being pampered.

"Come on Marston, don't make a meal of it," she joked. I was then taken to my hotel by taxi (Ann had to walk) and given a celebrity-style welcome at the hotel (as were all runners). I made my way to my room only to vomit down the toilet before having a shower and getting dressed for the award ceremony in the open air of the Town's Market Square.

And as we sat at the presentation on the evening of the finish in Sparta, we were all reminded that not only had we ran in a gruelling race but we had followed in the steps of an ancient messenger, a modern day Pheidippides if you like.

Tears of pride welled in my eyes as the organisers claimed that, "All of the athletes that had completed the distance can claim that by taking part in the race, in the eyes of Greek folk, they are almost a God."

Chapter Eleven
The Loneliness of a Long-Distance Runner

After a really eventful year, I was so looking forward to 2005, and as the New Year began, I was now training for the London Marathon, the Rome Marathon, the 145-mile Grand Union Canal and another seven-day World record attempt. The National Autistic Society had approached me to repeat my world record breaking attempt of running for seven days on a treadmill, but this time in a shop window at Lilywhites sports store in Piccadilly, London.

And now, I was to be performing to a huge audience and that audience was to be the London public, and so London was inviting me to perform and do what I do best…RUN.

The plan was to run on a treadmill for seven days and then run in the London Marathon on the eighth day. To break a world record is one thing but to run in the London Marathon as a 'lap of honour' was another. And so, I was hard in training as I tried to juggle my parental duties with keeping a job down and running in the toughest of challenges that the world has to offer.

I was now being presented with all kinds of awards and being invited to television shows and one in particular was about feeling younger than you are.

It was presented by Des Lynham and Emily Maitliss and I was so excited about being asked to be a guest on the broadcast, and that excitement was with me all the way down the M1 as I drove myself and Ann to the studio in Wembley, London.

I eventually reached the studio and was met with other guests before taking my place in front of the camera to be interviewed by Emily. I could not believe my luck, for there I was in the studio but instead of sitting with 'JOE PUBLIC' in the studio, I was sitting amongst celebrities such as 'Jane Seymour', 'Harry Rednap' and 'Richard Hammond' and then talking live on air about my running and about my challenges.

This was live and if I made a mistake, I would be made to look silly in front of the whole nation and this made my nerves even worse. But I didn't need to worry, for I was good in my performance and I spoke with confidence as I carried on about the joys of looking good and performing like a finely tuned athlete in my quests of achieving great goals in my sport.

March was soon upon us and I was flying from East Midlands Airport to Rome with my mate Sean. Sean was runner with Sneyd Striders, running until he had quit running to concentrate on setting up his own business of supplying X-ray equipment to hospitals of which he had come up with his own product. Unfortunately, I was feeling ill and had a burning sore throat, and as Sean and I booked into our hotel in Rome my voice was becoming weaker and weaker and I feared that I would be coming down with the flu! Now to run a marathon with a heavy cold or the flu was a stupid thing to do but I had come such a long way to run in this event and I wasn't going contemplate not turning up for the marathon.

Sean and I had the time of our lives as we visited local sites such as the Coliseum and the Trevi fountain. Rome is such a wonderful place to be, but for me I spent most of my holiday visiting chemist shops to buy medication for my condition and I must have visited almost every chemist in Rome.

On the morning of the marathon, I phoned Ann from my mobile but as I tried to talk, I could not utter a word as my throat was burning up and the coughing had started to become louder and louder.

Ann begged me, "Don't run today Glyn, you're too ill to run a marathon, so just stay in your room until Sean gets back from the race."

I managed to agree with her through my coughing but in reality, I could not stay in my room while a marathon was happening nearby. I got dressed into my running kit and made myself to Sean's room and then down to breakfast.

Sean and I ate a real athlete's breakfast which consisted of bacon, sausages, fried bread and a glass of orange juice for the vitamin C content of course.

We jogged our way to the Coliseum to the start of this grand event, as we got near to the start line, the crowds of runners and spectators got thicker and thicker. However, each time I coughed there would be an 'exclusion zone' around Sean and I and everyone would rush out of my way. The marathon went well, as well as could be expected for a runner with a heavy cold, and I was so delighted to have reached the finish line with a time of just under four hours. A slow time for me as a runner but under the circumstances a great achievement.

When I reached home, I was given a real hero's welcome and I showed off my marathon medal to a proud family, and of course I had a phone call from my local newspaper reporter asking me for my story of the marathon in Rome, of which I happily gave them.

I had no time to rest on my laurels, for I was soon planning my London challenge and the seven-day world record for running on a treadmill. With a right knee that was giving me some cause for concern, I was getting worried about the forthcoming challenge.

However, I had pledged to do this challenge and so quitting would not be an option; which is why I never went to seek medical advice, for if I was ordered not to run for a few months it would have meant letting my charity down and I couldn't do that. And so, 'the show must go on' attitude was adopted by myself for this event, stupid for me to take this attitude but it is how I am – 'do or die' that's me.

Starting on Sunday 10th of April (a week before the London Marathon), I was lining up to run for a whole week in the shop window of Lillywhites sports store in Piccadilly circus, London, then run the 26-mile London Marathon the day after finishing the seven-day treadmill challenge. I started at 9 am on the first day (Sunday), it felt strange to be running in a shop window with passers-by stopping to look at this strange man running on a treadmill. As the day wore on the crowds got bigger and so did the cheers, which gave me the encouragement to give more effort, which in turn helped me manage a respectable 49 miles on the first day. And with a sore knee I was so happy with the 49 miles I had ran, which meant that I was easy on for the world record, which was set at 283 miles. I got off the treadmill at 9 pm.

Monday morning, 9 am, I was back on the machine, people were passing the shop window, and despite being in a hurry to get to work, they still had time to shout words of encouragement (and donate to my chosen charity – The National Autistic Society), and with helpers from the charity on hand to shake buckets outside the shop, the fundraising was always going to be great.

Groups of tourists were stopping and snapping away with their cameras, which helped me to beat the tedious task of running in one spot all day. Treadmill running is boring, especially when you are used to pounding out the miles by hitting the roads, but my support crew from the National Autistic Society were fantastic, they kept me motivated and focused on my target to break the world record, but yet again my right knee had become quite sore as the day wore on, and so I was delighted to reach the end of the day but despite this I ran 51 miles bringing my total to 100 miles.

Tuesday started the same as the previous two days – get out of bed, shower, then into the dining room of my hotel for light breakfast, before heading off to Lilywhites cup of tea, then on the treadmill for another day's running, the folks passing by had got used to seeing me in the shop window and became an unofficial fan club-crowds would stop to look in the window and ask how far have I run, and how do I feel?

The truth was that I was feeling so concerned for my right knee which was painful from just walking the few yards from Piccadilly station to Lilywhites, but I continued to run with that do or die attitude of mine.

Different groups of people would stop to cheer and donate, the folks commuting to and from work would be more than willing to give me a bit of their time to cheer me onto a world record, and of course donate to the charity.

This event was more than breaking a world record, more than raising cash for the charity, but to raise awareness of Autism, and the great work that is done by 'The National Autistic Society', and of course they were overwhelmed by the publicity I was generating from the seven-day treadmill record. By 9 pm Tuesday evening, I had run 50 miles, giving me a total of 150 miles over the three days. I stepped off the treadmill and headed towards my hotel with a swollen right knee.

Wednesday, day four of this record attempt, and now the local media were buzzing about what was happening in Lillywhites window. I got a phone call at 7:30 am in my room, it was Danny Baker, presenter of a breakfast radio show.

This gave me the chance to publicise the work done for Autism by the charity, and to thank everyone for the support they have been giving me, especially the staff at Lillywhites, who looked in on me from time to time to check if I was okay, and to bring me food and drink. Danny asked, "How do you keep yourself motivated, and how do you beat the boredom of treadmill running?"

I explained that I was armed with my I-Pod and listened to my favourite tracks when this got tedious, and of course with myself being a huge fan of QUEEN, my I-Pod had got the full catalogue of Queen tracks on it.

Then Danny quipped, "I suppose the QUEEN track that sums you up would be 'Don't stop me now'."

"Too right," I replied, of which Danny played the track just after announcing that he would be popping down to Lillywhites to give my charity twenty quid.

This had given the start to the day that I needed, and I started with full motivation. The cheers from the public got bigger and better throughout the day, but an unexpected surprise was heading my way. A group of girls (whom had passed by each day) decided to give me one huge surprise, one of the young ladies flashed her boobs, if I had blinked, I would have missed it, it was that quick, however I never blinked, but I nearly fell off the treadmill!

I was now in real pain and with my right knee so swollen, I was forced to ask one of my support team to buy me a knee support, in the hope that it would give me some relief; and now, I was running with a huge white bandage tube around my joint and the worry of a seriously swollen knee.

And so with an eventful day over, another 50 miles had passed, bringing the total miles ran so far to 200 miles.

I returned to my hotel after stopping off at a shop to buy a bag of ice cubes and once in my room, I wrapped the bag of ice around my right knee to try to get the swelling down.

I spent all evening with the bag on my knee and it paid off for the swelling on my knee was greatly reduced by the time I went to bed.

Thursday (day 5), the usual start of the day, shower, breakfast, treadmill.

The money raised so far was looking good, people had been so generous and everyone who witnessed the challenge were in awe of what I was trying to achieve, in fact they felt privileged to be witnessing such an event. I had been hoping to run 50 miles a day, each day. But by now, I was slowing (but only a little) and a small red 'bruise' had appeared on the lower part of my right leg along with some slight pain, but was nothing to cause concern about at the moment. However, my right knee was swelling up again and becoming extremely painful.

The day had been great with support getting bigger, but news had been given to us that Kelly Holmes was on her way (as part of a publicity campaign for a top sports company).

The local press were there, as were the local television news presenters. While waiting for Kelly Holmes arrival, they flocked around my treadmill challenge – again great news for my charity and highlighting the work they do.

After the media interest had gone, I was given news that Kelly Holmes had said live on television, "Before I answer any questions, can I wish GLYN MARSTON all the very best in his record attempt, and I hope he reaches his target."

This filled me with a new enthusiasm, but I would have liked to have met Kelly Holmes instead of being stuck on a treadmill during her visit. But I was on a mission and I had no time to lose by queuing up for an autograph but then to my surprise, I was led to an upstairs office, where I met the lady herself, Kelly Holmes – Dame Kelly, large as life in front of me, and boy did she give me some useful advice about staying focused on my goal.

Today had been the best day ever, and even though I managed 45 miles (and not the 50 miles I had hoped for), I was still on a high and I had a total miles ran of 245 miles.

Concerns for my right knee were even more evident now as I was limping back to my hotel and walking was getting painful too.

Friday (day 6), I was feeling a little more pain. The small red bruise on my right leg had now got bigger and more painful, still I carried on with the record attempt, and with the support I was getting it was too easy to put this 'injury' out of my mind.

However, as I jogged my way to the record, my leg was getting worse and after stopping to apply some treatment, I was beginning to fear shin splints.

I had never had shin splints, I had knee injuries and swollen ankles, but never shin splints – can you get shin splints by running on a treadmill?

My right knee was swelling up and my support was in agreement to get a proper medical knee support to replace the bandage that had protected my right knee for the last few days. This allowed me to run through the world record by 8:15 on Friday evening, and I stepped off the treadmill to a thunderous applause by a huge crowd that had gathered outside, of course I went outside to thank 'my public' for the support.

I limped back to my hotel room and had a long soak in the bath.

With a total of 283.5 miles to my name, I had now broken the record.

Saturday was to be an easy run. I wanted to get to 300 miles then stop, this will be achieved by 12 noon, I predicted, but the right leg had caused some pain yet again, so I could only manage an hour of steady jogging, then stopped for a 15-minute rest followed by another hour of steady jogging and then a 15-minute rest and so on.

I eventually reached the 300 miles at 2:50 pm on Saturday, then I got off the treadmill for good! After thanking all the staff at Lillywhites for their kind offer of using their window, I set off for my hotel and took a longest soak in the bath before even thinking of tackling the London Marathon the next day.

Sunday 17th April, London Marathon.

For anyone who has never ran a marathon, the thought of running for 26 miles is a daunting prospect, so imagine running a marathon straight after running 300 miles in one week!

I was feeling tired, my legs were heavy and I was not looking forward to the marathon at all. I did set myself a target of reaching the finish line in under four and a half hours (when you consider that I ran last year's marathon in three hours and 22 minutes, this was showing just how much I had expected the treadmill record attempt to affect my running in the marathon).

I reached the finish line in a time of four hours and 15 minutes, and I had a sense of pride that I had raised £1,300 for the charity, and of course being a world record holder.

On my return home, I was now facing mixed emotions, for I was on a high for breaking the seven-day world treadmill record but on a low as my right leg was now hampering my training for the 145-mile Grand Union Canal Race. I managed to get rid of the redness on my lower right leg but my right knee was slightly bigger than my left knee.

Nigel Churchill and Steve Hill was in charge of the canal race support team, and as before each runner had taken it in turns to run a ten mile stretch of the canal towpath with me, but as each runner ended their stint with me, they reported to

Nigel and Steve that all was not well with me and I needed someone to 'kick my butt and get my mind focused on the race'!

This year's Grand Union Canal Race was a success but despite being faster than the previous year, I finished in fourth place.

At home, things were becoming a little tense and with my running friends at Sneyd Striders – that included female runners – which made Ann so angry. She started to question my motives for wanting to run so much, especially when I was suffering with a swollen right knee.

Ann gave me a barrage of accusations for almost every day of every week of every month which obviously led to arguments and in turn I would bring up my suspicions of her 'involvement' with Martin. But each time I accused her of having an affair, Ann would stare me in the eyes and reply with an instant denial of having an affair with Martin or any other man.

But one evening as I returned home from the running club, Ann decided to come clean and admit to an affair. I just sat down with my head in my hands as she told me her side of the story. "You have to understand that at the time we were facing issues with autism and you were off running all the time," she explained as she sobbed. "A guy at work, much younger than me was giving me a lot of attention and eventually, I gave in."

"Gave in, you gave in?" I questioned as my eyes were filling up.

"It started off as harmless flirting and then one day, he kissed full on the lips," sobbed Ann. "It went from there to stealing kisses when we could and touchy-feely kind of thing."

"Touchy, feely, foreplay to put it politely?" I sneered back.

"We only had sex once, just once and it was over quickly but I cried when we had finished. I was devastated that I had done what I did with another man, devastated that I had cheated on you and it was then I realised just how much I love you," cried Ann hysterically.

What could I do but cry, I slept on the settee that evening and cried myself to sleep and even though Ann came down to me in the early hours of the morning, she still couldn't console me, and I had no option but to phone in sick at work. I still refused to believe that Ann had only had sex with another man on one occasion and accused her constantly of 'doing it' more than once with this man, but she stuck to her story of feeling guilty after the one time, so guilty in fact that Martin was worried that she would break down and tell me what she had done, which is the reason he left his job and moved on.

I was now getting back into my training for the Spartathlon 2005 race in Greece and though I was trying to put the problem between Ann and me to one side and focus on my training, I was finding it difficult to forget what she had told me and sometimes I was finding it hard to forgive her too. I was now visiting the doctor on a regular basis and was prescribed antidepressants to help me through a difficult time of my life, and with a 153-mile race to take on it was all becoming too much for me to bear.

October 2005 and the Spartathlon race was upon me, and Ann had agreed to join me to give us a chance to be alone from everyone and start again but my head was spinning, as I tried to come to terms with the fact that my wife had submitted herself to another man. I would look at her and say nasty things to her and then I would apologise to her, only to insult her again soon afterwards.

I hated my wife and then I loved her, then I hated her and so it went on with my emotions going overboard and running wild in my head. The flight to Athens was a subdued one with myself and Ann hardly speaking to each other.

We reached our hotel and I registered for the race before making my way to the roof top swimming pool for a relaxing swim in the heat of a warm afternoon. Ann was trying her best to put our relationship back to how it was before she admitted her affair and I was happy to try again but at the same time, I wanted her to suffer for what she had done to me.

The morning of the race had arrived and we made our way to the start of the race and Ann asked me if I would propose to her at the finish line of the Spartathlon. "Just think of it, Glyn," she smiled. "What if you ask me to marry you at the foot of the King Leonidas in Sparta and in front of everyone too, wouldn't that be great?" laughed Ann.

"But we are already married," I replied in some confusion.

"We can renew our wedding vows but this time we will get married in a church," she announced.

So it was agreed that when I reached the finish of the race (some 35 hours later), I will call Ann upon the steps of the statue of King Leonidas and ask her to re-marry me.

But all was not as straight forward as it seemed, for as I ran the first sixty miles of the race, my right knee was so painful that I was actually crying in pain with every step I had taken. The evening was getting darker, the weather had taken a turn for the worse as we were caught in a downpour of torrential rain.

I was now running up the first mountain of the race and with the rain lashing at my face, I was feeling so deflated and beginning to regret turning up for this race but I still pushed on and gritted my teeth as the pain from my knee became more unbearable.

I was still crying from the pain of my right knee and with a constant uphill road to tackle, I was slowing up and became less enthusiastic about being in the race, in fact I was beginning to think, 'who cares about the finish line, I finished this race last year so I don't have anything to prove'. I ran for further thirty miles and was now down to a walk as my right knee was now completely swollen and so painful that I couldn't find the will to carry on in the race. At the 95-mile checkpoint, I walked up to a marshal and ripped my race number from my running top and handed it to the marshal (which signalled my intended retirement from the event). I stood there in a pathetic state in a downpour of rain, I was feeling deflated and I was feeling defeated as I handed my race number over.

The race marshal shook his head and shouted, "NO, NO, you must carry on for you are Glyn Marston, Glyn Marston never quits a race…never," he stated as he tried to give me back my race number.

But I was adamant and I walked to the coach that was waiting nearby to take early retired runners to Sparta. I sat on the coach with my head hung low and feeling sorry for myself, as I thought about letting Ann down, for if I didn't make it to the finish line and I couldn't ask her to marry me. But then again, why should I get down on one knee for Ann, renewing our wedding vows will only be for Ann's benefit, for it will be a way of putting a line under everything and starting anew.

I reached our hotel room in Sparta at two o'clock in the morning and gently knocked on the door. Ann answered and looked at me with sorrow in her eyes, for she knew just how hard quitting a race would be for me to bear (even though I had run over 95 miles nonstop).

"My knee gave way on me and then we had torrential rain to contend with too which was too much for me to take on and so I quit at 95 miles," I sighed as I stripped off my running gear.

I jumped in to the shower and then went to bed and quickly fell asleep, only to be woken up by Ann with a cup of tea in her hand. "Drink that Glyn and you'll feel a lot better," chirped Ann.

"Feel better with a cup of tea?" I quizzed. "How can I feel better, I have failed to reach the finish line and it's your fault," I snapped as I jumped out of bed and into the bathroom.

"How is it my fault?" Ann asked. "You can't blame me for your knee giving out on you and as for the rain, is that my fault too," she sarcastically asked.

And she was correct for how could I blame her for the weather and as for my right knee, well it wasn't her fault that it was so swollen, was it?

But the truth is that I had taken on the world's most gruelling challenges and became victorious. I had done all of it despite being sick and vomiting on some races, despite running 145 miles nonstop only two weeks after having my leg out of a plaster cast and despite my right knee swelling badly on the seven-day world treadmill record challenge (and being on medication for life to control epilepsy). I had still completed the task and finished the challenge in hand because of my mental strength, but now I had lost all that was positive in my mind. I was now wilting away with my confidence diminishing – and it was all of Ann's doing, she was responsible for my world falling apart, so I thought.

When we returned to Athens, my mood was somewhat subdued as I contemplated the thought of telling my mates that I had failed in this year's Spartathlon, of course Ann reassured me that I had proved myself on the previous year's Spartathlon by reaching the finish line. I had nothing to prove and anyway, my right knee was never going to allow me to run the whole 153 miles anyway, so I was stupid to have even entered this year's race.

We were invited to the presentation in Athens and though I had not reached the finish line, I still attended so I could cheer the successful athletes on the race who had reached the finish line, and as we sat at our tables a pretty Grecian woman smiled at me as she walked toward our table.

"Who is she?" Ann asked.

"I don't know," I whispered as I smiled back at the woman.

"She seems to know you," grunted Ann.

"But I don't know her," I replied as I was staring at a woman whom was gazing back at me. As the woman walked behind me, she ran her fingers up my back and along my neck, only to gently rub my ear as she passed by.

This angered Ann and it started an argument between ourselves. When we reached our hotel room in Athens, Ann was so convinced that I had met this woman while I was on the race and though I pleaded my innocence, it made no difference, and therefore we were back to square one, with me calling Ann all sorts of names and cursing her for having an affair with Martin.

When we returned home, we were arguing again but this time Ann was not so keen on trying to save her marriage and was now telling me to leave if I didn't want to forgive her for her affair. We were back to the point where I would sleep on the settee and ignoring Ann whenever I could.

As my life was spiralling out of control, I was forced to seek advice from my doctor whom prescribed medication for my depression, yes I was now suffering from severe depression and my mood swings were making me angrier and angrier. My training was beginning to suffer too as I would get to a few miles in a training run and fall to the ground. My right knee would just give way and could not support me on some training runs and the thought of having to stop the one thing I was passionate about was making me more depressed.

It wasn't long after I had discovered the truth about Ann and Martin that I had started to go out on training runs alone, for there were many days that I felt I couldn't face the world, I felt so alone.

I was now going through the worse part of my life as I felt that I hadn't got a friend in the world, nobody to trust anymore and no-one that I could confide in. I started to keep myself to myself by putting up a barrier, a barrier that would keep me safe from those who want to do me harm.

After a few weeks, I was now doing things on my own as if I were a single man. Ann had thrown our marriage away some ten years ago so why not act as a bachelor?

And so I would go to the pub on my own, go out on my motorbike for a long ride or go to town and do some clothes shopping on my own, and it was in a shop in Walsall that a voice whispered in my ear, "Hello Marston."

Turning quickly, I looked at the woman who was standing in front of me, "JANE, JANE HOW THE HELL ARE YOU?" I yelled in delight.

"How long as it been," replied Jane as we hugged each other. "It must be over thirty-two years now," said Jane as she pondered in her mind when we last met. "1977, when we split up as I recall," she said. "You know when you were having epilepsy," she went on.

"I am on medication for life but my last seizure was in 1977," I replied. "Errm yes…what about going to McDonalds for a coffee or a tea?" I suggested,

"Okay then, a cup of tea and a Mcflurry too," she laughed. "Okay and a Mcflurry too," I smirked in reply as I was so pleased to see Jane again, and boy did she look great, for she hadn't aged that much and looked so pretty.

We sat in McDonalds and told each other our stories and what we had been up to over the years.

I told her my story of my marriage on the rocks and Jane went on to tell me her story, "Well, I got married to a man whose dad was a successful business man and he gave his son everything he wanted and he became a spoilt sod, but when we were married, he expected me to be his wife, mother, nurse, cleaner and house slave," Jane told me. "But when I started to say make your own cup of tea or clean it up yourself, he got violent and would punch me. It got so bad that he put me in hospital and I had to say that I fell over the dog who was laying on the landing and I fell from the top of the stairs to the bottom," explained Jane as tears were welling in her eyes.

I wrapped my arms around her and said, "Please don't cry, anyway you'll dilute your Mcflurry if you get it too wet."

Jane giggled as she wiped the tears from her eyes and then she stared me in the eyes and we kissed there and then. I never thought that I could get so excited over one kiss but kissing another woman after being in one relationship for twenty-five years was a thrill.

I returned home in a totally different mood than I had been in over the past few weeks. I would go to the local pub for a drink and spend most of the evening sending Jane text messages and she would reply, but as the evening wore on the cheeky text messages were turning into sex messages as we were both telling each other what we wanted to do to each other and what would happen if we were ever alone together.

One Sunday morning (a chilly November morning) when I was on a planned twenty-mile training run, I was forced to walk yet again due to the pain in my right leg (my right knee was swollen). As I walked along feeling sorry for myself a car pulled up alongside me. "Do you know, you have one hell of a sexy ass Mr Marston," called Jane from her car as she wound down her car window.

"Bloody hell Jane," I panted as I slowed down to a walking pace, "Were you just passing or are you stalking me?" I joked.

"OOH, I'd be happy to stalk you wherever you go," chuckled Jane. "Why are you walking?" she asked. "Do you need a lift?"

I went over to her car and got inside, well I limped into her car as she looked at my knee. "Bloody hell mate, you need to get that sorted," she said as she touched my knee. "I can take you home or you can come to my house, I have some ice for your knee."

And though I knew that the issue with my right was way beyond the help of any ice pack, I agreed to go to her house and as we walked into the hallway, closing the front door behind me, Jane just kissed me so passionately with her hands running all over my body and exploring every inch of me. I responded in the same way and before long we were both semi naked as we made our way up the stairs and into a bedroom. The moment was magic and it was the first time that I had made love in ages, but then came the realisation of what I had now done to my wife, and though she had done the same to me some ten years previously, two wrongs don't make a right. Eventually Jane drove me home, well, she dropped me off around the corner, and as I walked into the house, I got a barrage of questions from Ann.

"Where have you been until now?" Ann asked. "Your dinner will be ruined by now," she said as she took out a Sunday roast from the oven that was now a little crispy on the top.

"Sorry, but I ended up walking again," I replied as to cover the truth behind the day's events and Jane.

But eventually my guilt got the better of me and I was to admit what I had done. Ann just stared at me with tears running down her face. "I deserve it, I deserve it," she cried.

"I am sorry, so sorry," I sobbed as I sat on the floor with my head in my lap.

Was this the nail in our coffin, the end of our marriage?

And though I wanted to get away from my home, my wife and my current situation, I was still hopeful that a solution from anywhere would save us.

Chapter Twelve
The End?

What I had with Jane was exciting but the guilt was now taking over the thrill of sex with another woman, and so it also brought with it the questions from Ann. She would question my whereabouts if I was home late. Jane was still texting me and refusing to let me have a 'one off' love-making session with her, she made it clear that she wanted us to be in a permanent relationship.

And though, I was struggling to run long distances, I agreed to enter the Rome Marathon again and take Ann along for a long break. My family agreed to look after the children while we were away as to give us time to put our problems behind us.

My running buddy, Sean, had asked if he and his girlfriend could come along too as he wanted run in the Rome Marathon for the second year in a row too. And so in the hope of us making it up and putting our pasts behind us, I signed up for the Rome Marathon which was early March. And now, my training routine had become even more intense, for I was now into my training for the London Marathon (April) and the 145-mile Grand Union Canal (May) too. But next year instead of running on a treadmill for seven days to break the world seven-day treadmill record, I decided to organise a 'TEAM SEVEN DAY WORLD RECORD ATTEMPT', where a team of twelve runners would take it in turns to run on a treadmill over a seven-day period and then run in London Marathon on the final day. This would ease the pressure that I was feeling from the prospect of telling the National Autistic Society that I would be unable to run in Lilywhites window as I had done the previous year, and so the fundraising event was now arranged. All I had to do is find my team of runners.

This was easy as I had a number of keen runners wishing to be part of the team and so my team were fellow Sneyd Striders runners – Colin Highfield, Stan Harrison, Sean Haydon, Phil Gelder, Steve Budjoso, my son Liam and myself and we were to be accompanied by Kathy Hearn (a fellow ultra-distance runner) and a writer from Running Fitness magazine by the name of Ryan Bowd, who would write up a story of the event on his 'CHALLENGE THE GUINEA PIG' page.

Ryan Bowd was a Canadian triathlete who had set himself up as a real-life guinea pig and was inviting readers to challenge him to take on any running event in the country or even the whole world, and so I had written to the magazine to challenge him to be part of my world record breaking team.

I was getting increasingly concerned about my right knee but I refused to get medical advice in the fear of being told that I would have to quit my running forever, and so I would pop a few painkillers as I ran on my training sessions. Jane had now become a stalker and she would drive around the areas that she knew I would be running, and so bad was her stalking that I had been forced to run along the canal towpaths to avoid her. A few months was to pass before we would ever meet again, and part of me wanted to meet Jane again but part of me wanted to try and make up with my wife. But eventually I met up with Jane to tell her that I was giving my marriage another try. "It won't work; once the trust and respect has gone from a relation, a break up is definite," Jane said in a bold tone.

However, I tried to make it up to Ann and went along with the scenario of playing happy families as not to spoil our time in Rome. As for the marathon, I ran along with Sean for about six miles until my knee had become so painful that I was forced to walk for a short while, and I asked Sean to carry on and run his own race and I would see him at the finish line.

I limped my way through the route of the marathon as I became more of a tourist than an athlete in the race. I would run for a few miles and then walk for a mile to ease the pain in my knee and by the time I had reached the eighteen miles of the marathon, I was in tears as the pain had become too intense to put up with.

As I limped along the route, I heard a voice call out, "GLYN, GLYN ARE YOU OKAY?" It was Ann yelling out to me.

"DO I LOOK LIKE I AM OKAY?" I yelled back.

I walked over to where Ann was standing and she passed me a few painkillers. "Get them down you Glyn, they may help you reach the finish line," she said.

And so, I quickly gulped down the pills with a quick sip of my energy drink from the running bottle that I always carried in my left hand as I ran and it did the trick, for I was slowly picking up my pace as the pain was beginning to ease and the next six miles passed so quickly. But as I reached the twenty-four-mile marker of the marathon, my pain returned with a vengeance and the pain that I had eased by taking painkillers was feeling ten times worse as the effects of the pills were wearing off.

Those last two miles of the marathon were the worst moments of my life as I felt that I was being violently stabbed in my right knee, and so I hobbled toward the finish line. Another two marathon runners offered to support me by putting their arms under my arms and allow me to run with no pressure or impact on my legs, but being a proud long-distance runner, I thanked them for their concern and explained that I wanted to cross the finish line on my own steam.

I crossed the finish line and then slumped to the ground in tears. Sean was quick to be by my side and helped to my feet.

"Come on buddy, let's get back to the hotel and get changed and then paint the town red," he laughed as he tried to cheer me up.

Alas, it wasn't long before our Rome holiday was over and we were making our way home and back to reality, we had missed the kids (even though Louise was 18 years old, she was still a kid to us). I was now training Liam to run and he became a regular at Sneyd Striders running club and was running in distances of six miles and at a good pace too. It was obvious that he was enjoying his new found hobby and his club mates were in awe of his ability and his fast pace.

Apart from running and working, I was now busying myself with the organisation of the 'Team Seven Day World Treadmill Record Challenge' at Lilywhites store in London's Piccadilly. There was great media interest that surrounded the challenge and my time was spent conducting interviews with local and national newspapers, radio stations and television news programmes.

At this time, I received the weirdest request that I had ever heard, to run in the London Marathon...dressed as BATGIRL!

Phil Bant (a fellow National Autistic Society fundraiser) had planned to run the 2006 London Marathon dressed as batman alongside his friend, who would be dressed as Robin but the woman who had agreed to dressed up as Batgirl was now injured and had pulled out of the London Marathon.

Phil had submitted a story to the local media about the trio of super heroes (and heroine) running in the London Marathon, and therefore needed another person to run with him as Batgirl. It sounded like fun and so I agreed and went out and bought a BATGIRL costume.

Fortunately, for myself, I had the seven-day treadmill world record to look forward to, the London Marathon and the Grand Union Canal Race too. Thank God for my running, because without it I would be a man with nothing to live for, and therefore I needed my thrill of ultra-distance running to keep me alive.

And so, I was challenging for another entry into the Guinness book of records, along with my friends from my running club. The time was soon upon us and it didn't seem too long before we were driving to London and the world record challenge. Liam was so excited to be going to London, for he enjoyed his trips on the underground trains when he visited London before and he couldn't wait to ride on the tube once again.

So following the success of my seven-day treadmill world record challenge at Lilywhites store in London the previous year, I was welcomed back again to repeat the challenge once again.

However, even though the thought of running for seven days on a treadmill and then tackling the London Marathon on the eighth day was so inviting, I thought that this year I was in need of help, for my right knee was never going to allow me to run such a gruelling event on my own.

So after contacting Guinness World Records about a team seven-day treadmill world record attempt, I set about putting the team together for another world record challenge in the shop window of Lilywhites.

The rules were, no more than twelve runners to be allowed in the team and only one runner at any one time can be running during the challenge, simple!

My team still consisted of fellow Sneyd Striders running club members, who were: Stan Harrison, Colin Highfield, Phil Gelder, Steve Budjoso, Sean Haydon, myself and my son Liam (of whom would be celebrating his 15th Birthday during the event), the other two members that made up the team were a fellow ultra (and Grand Union Canal) runner, Kathy Hearn and Ryan Dowd (a triathlete and a member of Running Fitness Magazine production team). I know that this made a team of nine runners but the rules were 'no more than 12 runners'.

Now to be honest, there were no record set for this challenge, so we would be setting a world record for others to beat. The charity we were raising funds for was again a charity close to my heart – The National Autistic Society (NAS), of whom were so wonderful in publicising the whole event. It was also agreed that the challenge was to be started on the Friday as to maximise publicity.

Now the team at NAS came up with a name for our team of runners and that name was 'TEAM ENDEAVOUR', of whom I was captain. This was a great moment for myself as I was running with a team instead of a solo attempt, and to be in London with my mates certainly made the attempt a whole more exciting.

As the week went on, we had a fan club of spectators who would stop and watch for a while but it was to be the final minutes of the challenge that were to be my proudest, for Liam was to be the last runner, the one runner to run over the finish line so to speak.

Liam stepped up to the treadmill and as he was setting his pace, a crowd had gathered outside the store window to cheer Liam over the 'finish line', but as the minutes ticked by, the crowd had doubled as passers-by joined the team from Lilywhites to cheer this great young runner who will close the challenge.

Liam gave his cheeky smile to the crowd as usual but this was added with a wink, to which the crowd gave a huge, "AAHH bless him." As the final minutes ticked away the crowd started to chant, "LIAM, LIAM, LIAM." I stood outside with my camera snapping away, I was getting a little emotional as I watched with pride as my son started to play up to the attention he was getting. As the crowd started to count down from 10, Liam gave a huge wave to his audience, at that point tears welled in my eyes. I think almost everyone there became emotional at this point, it was a proud moment for me, even more so when Liam stopped the treadmill and stood to face a crowd of cheering onlookers.

I thought that he may have become a little distressed by the noise and commotion he had caused, but no, he soaked up the entire accolade and applause so much that we had to tell him that he could stop waving and blowing kisses to his fans if he wanted, not bad for a kid with autism.

Eventually, we got to the tube station and prepared for our journey home, and all the way up the motorway, Liam was asking of how he did and could he do it again next year – great signs that he could be following in his father's footsteps and a running career, who knows?

We arrived home to a proud mother (and wife) and Ann had saved all the newspaper stories that had been published about the challenge. Liam was full of tales of his time in London and begged that we take him again for a short break.

Saturday morning and I was driving to London yet again for the London Marathon. Myself and Nigel Churchill accompanied Dick Johnson to our hotel in the Capitol where we followed our usual London Marathon ritual of visiting the London Marathon expo on the Saturday afternoon, followed by a shandy at a pub on the evening and then waking up for the London Marathon the next morning. Sunday morning and the usual getting our running kits on and Nigel had noticed that I wasn't my usual chatting self.

"You okay buddy?" Nigel asked.

"Yeah, I'm fine mate," I sighed in response.

"No, you're not, Glyn," replied Nigel. "How about sharing them with me?" he continued.

"Sharing what?" I asked.

"Your thoughts mate, there is something on your mind, so talk to me, I can help you," demanded Nigel.

But the truth was that no one could help me, for I was feeling depressed (despite being on the happy pills that my doctor had prescribed) and my knee had swollen so much it was like a barrage balloon.

Despite wearing a knee support, my joint was now beginning to get even worse than ever and I was now limping when I walked, let alone when I ran.

"Look mate, I have had a long, long week with the treadmill event and I guess I am feeling tired mate," I explained to Nigel as I tried to hide my real feelings.

"Lying git," snapped Nigel, "But your choice, if you want to suffer alone then so be it, but you know where I am if you need me," explained my good friend.

We made our way to Blackheath (with me dressed as Batgirl) for the start of the marathon. The starting area of the London Marathon had its usual buzzing atmosphere as runners from all over the world were gathered for one of the greatest events in the long-distance runner's calendar, and as for myself, I had done this event for twelve years in succession (this being my thirteenth time in a row).

But this year was different as I was getting worried about how long I was going to take to reach the finish line at the mall, or would I reach the finish line?

My knee had been known to give way on me while I was in training (and without warning too), so what if the same happened on the race?

For the first time in my running career, I was actually worried about running a twenty-six-mile marathon but hey, this is the London Marathon and if I had to walk half the distance, then walk I will do, as long as I finish before those runners in the heavy Rhino costumes!

The first seven miles were a breeze and though my knee felt stiff, I still managed a good pace and held my head high as I ran with the usual pride that comes from a long-distance runner who had made a name for himself from his achievements.

However, during the fourteenth mile onwards, I was feeling the effects of a badly damaged knee and I knew that it would be only a matter of time before I go crashing to the ground from the crippled joint that had been plaguing my performance recently.

I ran, jogged and then walked for quite some time in a desperate bid to ease the pain in my right knee but I was suffering so much that I had decided to get medical advice as soon as I got home. But before then, I had a marathon to complete and with the final six miles ahead of me it was going to be a difficult task as I limped toward the finish line.

Finally, I had made it to the finish line and gratefully collected my marathon medal before making my way to my hotel and then the long drive home. The limp back to my hotel was a long and slow journey as I made my way through London with my head dropped on my chest, and instead of my usual happy attitude having just ran a great marathon event, I was feeling depressed again as I was contemplating the beginning of the end of my running career.

As Dick drove up the M1 motorway, he was chatting away about his finest performance to date on any marathon that he had ever ran. "Three hours and two minutes, what a run, a great day for me, a really incredible race," chirped a proud runner.

I sat in the back of the car with my aching leg stretched out on the seats and my head rested back against the door window.

"You need to get that sorted mate," sighed Nigel, "AND DON'T GIVE ME THAT SHIT THAT YOU'RE OKAY AND IT WILL PASS, BECAUSE YOU ARE ON THE VERGE OF CRIPPLING YOURSELF FOR LIFE IF YOU DON'T GET THAT KNEE LOOKED AT," demanded Nigel.

Nigel was correct in the fact that I could seriously damage myself but running was not a hobby or a pastime, to me it was an addiction and one I craved about for so long.

Even my wife was concerned and Ann would plead, "Glyn, Glyn," she pleaded, "Please take a break from your running and give your joints a rest before you end up in a wheelchair, please."

"But I have the Grand Union Canal Race to take on, I cannot miss out on running the canal race," I explained.

"The canal race, the whole 145 miles of the Grand Union Canal, from Birmingham to London, with a dodgy knee, you are mad, Marston...really mad," sighed Ann in disbelief as she couldn't understand why my running meant so much to me that I would risk my wellbeing before quitting my ultra-distance challenges.

With only six weeks until the Grand Union Canal Race, I was still in race mode as I had been training for the 145-mile run from Birmingham to London with Colin, but I wasn't looking forward to the race to be honest and the thought of being the only runner to have successfully completed the distance for five years in a row was not going to bettered by me completing six years in succession, but I will give it my best.

The morning of the race, I was being driven with Colin to Gas Street Basin in Birmingham and to the start of the 145-mile Grand Union Canal Race. I was just sat in the back of the support van and was unusually quiet.

We reached Gas Street and I was surrounded straight away by fellow runners who knew of my reputation on this race, "Going for gold this year Glyn," came the calls from the other competitors, "First place this year mate?" I was being asked as I made my way to registration. Everyone knew that I had finished in fourth place on two occasions, third place on two occasions and a second-place finish on this race and that I was hungry for first place and so I was the man to watch out for on the event. But what my fellow competitors didn't know was that my right knee may not make the distance and for the first on any race that I had ran, I was relying on luck rather than strength and endurance.

Dick Kearn sounded the horn to signal the start of the race and as usual we all ran at a steady pace for the first few miles, and the first ten miles went well and I was feeling good and more importantly, I was feeling confident too but how long will my knee last out – will I make the distance and reach the finish line in London.

I was fifth place on the race right up to the thirty-eight-mile point of the race where my knee gave way and sent me crashing to the ground. I screamed as I tried to pull myself to my feet. After about two miles, I walked up to where my support team were waiting and they were ready with support bandages and a cup of tea.

"I can't do it, I can't carry on," I told my support team as I grimaced in pain, the pain that was coming from my right knee, but they were not going to let me give up that easily and I was offered a few painkillers to get me back in the race and I reluctantly swallowed them and gulped them down with a last sip of my tea.

I set off along the towpath and was hoping to catch up on lost time and catch up with Colin whom I had urged to go on ahead, but I was in pain as I quickly walked, after a while the pain eased and in turn I was jogging on my way, after a few miles that jogging had turned into a fast-paced run as the pain from my knee was gone and I was running pain free.

I felt great and was running confidently until…THUD!

I was flat out on the towpath again as my knee had given way without warning. The painkillers had hidden the pain but they couldn't stop the repercussions of running with a damaged joint and by now my knee was swollen so big that it had turned purple under the strain of the race. I got to my feet and started jogging as I watched runners disappear in the distance. As the pain began to return to my knee, I was hopping along the towpath in a desperate bid to stay in the race but again I fell to the ground as my knee collapsed on me time and time again.

Eventually, I sat on a lock and pulled my mobile phone from my pocket and after dialling Nigel's mobile phone, I waited for a reply. "Hello mate, it's Glyn...I am quitting the race...I cannot continue with this pain, come and pick me up...please," I asked as I began to cry.

"STOP THAT BLOODY SOBBING," replied Nigel, "I am not letting you quit, so get your arse to Stoke Bruene and I'll fix you up," and on that the phone went dead. He had hung up!

I got to my feet as my anger had taken over the pain in my knee and I went almost sprinting along the towpath until I reached the support team at Stoke Bruerne.

"Nigel you git, I am in pain here and I cannot go on anymore," I panted as I slowed to a walking pace as I neared my team, but they were having none of my giving up attitude, for they knew that I would beat myself up over quitting the race for a long time to come if they let me give up too easily.

I had a change of clothes and a long sit down and my support team treated me like a racing car in a pit stop, where I had a group of supporters massaging me, washing my face with a warm damp flannel and someone placing a heat pad on my knee in a bid to ease the pain of my knee. And as I had refused any more painkillers, a heat pad was the only option available to me. Colin Highfield had run on ahead as he had his own race to run – he was to make it to the finish line on his very first 145-mile canal race, but for me the race had become a battle.

I ran from Stoke Bruerne for another five miles and through the seventy-mile checkpoint of the race and as I was way behind the time of my previous year's race, I had a lot of work to do to get myself back in the race – if I could get myself back in the race that is!

The one rule of this year's race was that no runner was allowed a running buddy until after the seventy-mile checkpoint and so at this checkpoint Nigel had waited for me to arrive so he could run alongside me.

"You do know that you are over four hours behind your time on last year's race?" he asked as we ran off along the towpath.

"YES, I BLOODY KNOW," I replied in disappointment of my performance on the race.

As I ran with Nigel, I kept falling to the ground as my knee gave way to me again and this happened time and time again in such a short distance until I went flying across the towpath. "I can't go on anymore mate," I sobbed to Nigel and as he pulled me to my feet. I just fell to the ground again and sat in the middle of the towpath with my head in my lap.

It must have been a funny sight to see a fully grown man in the wee dark hours of a Sunday morning sitting on the damp towpath and crying his eyes out as his mate was shouting, "SHUT UP, SHUT UP. You are showing yourself up by crying like a baby." Nigel helped me to a nearby lock where he sat me down and I was now screaming in pain as I lay along the lock in a bid to ease the pain in my leg.

Nigel had reached for his phone and called the race head office.

"Hello it's Glyn Marston's support team here…Yes, it is Nigel…Glyn has been forced to retire from the race, his knee is in a bad way and he can't carry on…yes we have reached the ninety-two-mile point of the race and he cannot continue…yes I will pass on your wishes. Thank you, goodbye," Nigel reported to the race organisers.

"They cannot believe you are quitting the race," Nigel told me. "They even gave me the option of letting you rest for a while before letting you carry on in the race," Nigel explained.

"I cannot go on mate, I just can't…I am finished," I sobbed.

"Well you can always run it again next year," Nigel reassured to me as he patted my head.

"No mate, when I said I am finished, I meant I am finished for good, for I fear that I screwed up my right knee...permanently," I cried as I was beginning to realise that my running career was almost over.

Nigel called our support team to get someone to drive over and pick us up and while we were waiting for my lift, Nigel and I chatted about the old days at Sneyd Striders running club.

"You have put our club on the map Glyn, Sneyd Striders have been featured in a running magazine, a BBC documentary and local news, including television news programmes. You must be the most famous non-celebrity in the country mate," grinned Nigel as he showed his pride of being part of my running challenges. "I am a better man because of you mate, so proud to tell everyone that I have helped Glyn Marston on most of his achievements," Nigel explained. And to be honest, Nigel Churchill was a dedicated friend and one of only a few people I knew I could trust.

As we sat there a few runners ran past us who looked surprised to see Glyn Marston sitting down on a race but they were pleasantly surprised to be passing me on the race.

As I cheered each runner on, I turned to Nigel and said, "I wouldn't have achieved any of that without your help mate and that of Sneyd Striders," I sighed as I continued with my thanks. "Apart from the Spartathlon, the Paris to London run and the Grand Canyon Rim to Rim challenge, you and Sneyd have been with me all the way," I smiled as I recalled my quests in ultra-distance running in a kind of eulogy as I was realising that my running was now dead, and on that our support van pulled up to the towpath.

I returned home and broke down in tears as I was forced to admit that my running days are over and my life was never to be the same. I did hope that perhaps there is one more chance, just one more chance for me to run again, maybe my knee is not as badly damaged as I thought it was.

Maybe, just maybe I will be running for many years to come.

The next day was the bank holiday Monday and a concerned wife woke me up and demanded, "Get dressed, I am taking you to the hospital to get that knee looked at," she called as she threw some clothes at me.

"Hang on a bit," I answered, "I haven't had a cuppa yet, I am not leaving here with a cup of tea inside me," I demanded as I hobbled downstairs and into the kitchen to put the kettle on.

Ann pushed me into the living room and bellowed, "Get dressed and I will make your tea for you, you can drink it in the car," Ann ordered.

The drive to the hospital was an experience as I tried to sip my tea without spilling any on my lap. "Bloody hell Ann, take it easy, unless you want accident and emergency to treat me for a scalded willy too," I ranted.

"Shut up moaning Marston and drink your tea," replied Ann as she raced to the hospital and I was desperately trying to keep the tea inside the mug without spilling it on my genitals.

We sat patiently and waited for my name to be called and as I was called, I hobbled into a cubicle helped by Ann and lay on a trolley. It wasn't too long before a doctor came to look at me and after bending my knee, he demanded an x-ray of my knee.

And so another long wait in the queue, for the x-ray department was ahead of me; that was followed by another wait for the doctor to return.

"Okay Mr Marston, you have a damaged cartilage to repair in that right knee but I am concerned about the swelling of your knee and the clicking of your knee as I bent it earlier. I am booking you an appointment to have arthroscopic surgery to repair your knee and at the same time to probe deeper into your joint to see what's going on in there but in the meantime, you have to rest, no running for a while!"

I waited for a few weeks before I got a letter to confirm my appointment for the arthroscopy surgery on my knee and

I would be a day patient, where I would go to theatre and have the treatment on my knee and hopefully be up and running within a month afterwards. But the news was devastating, I had damaged my right knee beyond repair and I was actually running with bone rubbing against bone as my cartilage was completely worn away.

I was to have my right knee completely replaced with a titanium joint and I would never be able to run again (unless I wanted to risk spending my life in a wheelchair).

And as I lay on a hospital bed with my right knee completely replaced with a titanium joint and the thought of never being able to run again, a nurse asked, "To almost cripple yourself in the name of running and for the sake of ultra-distance running, was it worth it?" To which I replied,

"Well, I have run across the Grand Canyon, ran in races of 150 miles, ran in numerous marathons around the world, broken world records for running on treadmills and met Her Majesty the queen...

"...HEY YEAH, IT WAS WORTH IT!"